Be a Champion of Youth

Genuine recycled paper with 10% post-consumer waste. 3827

The publishing team included Laurie Delgatto, development editor; Lorraine Kilmartin, reviewer; prepress and manufacturing coordinated by the production departments of Saint Mary's Press.

Copyright © 2007 by Saint Mary's Press, Christian Brothers Publications, 702 Terrace Heights, Winona, MN 55987-1318, www.smp.org. All rights reserved. No part of this book may be reproduced by any means without the written permission of the publisher.

Printed in the United States of America

ISBN 978-0-88489-939-6

Library of Congress Cataloging-in-Publication Data

Wilson McCarty, Maggie.
  Be a champion of youth : standing with, by, and for young people / Maggie Wilson McCarty, Robert J. McCarty.
    p. cm.
ISBN 978-0-88489-939-6 (pbk.)
  1. Church work with youth—Catholic Church. 2. Youth—Political activity. 3. Human rights advocacy. I. McCarty, Robert J. II. Title.
BX2347.8.Y7W56 2007
259'.23—dc22

                              2006035555

Be a Champion of Youth
Standing With, By, and For Young People

Maggie Wilson McCarty, DMin
Robert J. McCarty, DMin

Saint Mary's Press®

Author Acknowledgments

Because the young people at Saint Francis of Assisi Parish in Fulton, Maryland, and all the young people with whom we've ministered nationally and internationally, remind us that young people are gifts to be shared . . .

And because our adult colleagues continually work to ensure that the voice of the young Church is heard . . .

And because our ministry journey has been filled with companions who encouraged our voices . . . it was important to write this book.

To each of you, we say, thank you!

Contents

Introduction 6

1   What Is Advocacy? 9

2   Advocacy: Youth Participation 28

3   Forging Collaborative Partnerships 46

4   A Process for Advocacy. 53

5   Advocacy: Practical Strategies 66

6   Training for Advocacy 81

Appendix 91

Acknowledgments. 101

Introduction

We all know that the majority of young people today are leading healthy lives—studying, worshiping, working, volunteering, and playing positive roles in their communities. All too often though, they are portrayed in a negative light. Media headlines emphasize drug and alcohol abuse among youth, teen pregnancy, the rise in youth gangs, or school dropout rates—and often leave it at that. Even when the media's message about youth is positive, it often conveys the idea that youth are "the leaders of tomorrow." Such thinking obscures the fact that young people are already making solid contributions to others—tutoring younger children, protecting the environment, starting their own businesses, and leading new initiatives to improve their communities.

Advocacy helps to generate a respect for youth and their issues among parishioners, business owners, Church leaders, elected officials, policy makers, and key community leaders. Advocacy is a mind-set. It is about being a champion for young people. Advocacy is about speaking on behalf of young people, standing beside them in support of their causes, and helping them make a difference in the lives of others. Advocacy for youth means making a commitment to stand with, by, and for young people.

Yet the component of advocacy is the least understood and most overlooked aspect of ministry with young people. Certainly, advocacy is the component of youth ministry for which the fewest resources have been created. In fact, this is the first book of its kind that fully explores and unpacks the idea of youth advocacy as a ministry.

How This Book Came to Be

This book has been a long time in the making. What started out as a two-hour workshop for local parish youth ministers later expanded to a full-day training session for parish teams as part of a series of trainings on the components of youth ministry. The workshop then led to a chapter on advocacy in the book *The Vision of Catholic Youth Ministry: Fundamentals, Theory, and Practice,* published by Saint Mary's Press in 2005. And finally, Saint Mary's Press invited us to put our thoughts about and experience with advocacy into a book to help others understand the component more fully. The task has proved to be quite a challenge. Being an advocate for young people—and sharing this philosophy in a workshop—is one thing. Breaking down the aspects of advocacy to explain it to others in written form took a great deal of time and careful reflection and research. The result is a book intended to better educate ministry leaders so that they may be motivated to implement stronger and more effective advocacy efforts within their parishes and within the larger communities. *Be a Champion of Youth: Standing With, By, and For Young People* explores advocacy as an essential component of a comprehensive and life-changing Catholic youth ministry. This book can serve as a primer for individual coordinators of youth ministry to gauge their own advocacy efforts, or it may form the basis for empowering an entire youth ministry team or parish. The book can also serve as a valuable tool for independent or group study with parish staffs, ministry volunteers, parish leaders, and young people themselves. Here is what you will find:

Chapter 1 defines advocacy and provides the various contexts for the component. The chapter also includes a discussion on advocacy as an intentional and infused ministry to, by, for, and with young people, and provides some basic guiding principles for effective advocacy.

Chapter 2 describes the various levels of participation available to young people and offers some thoughts about adults' attitudes regarding youth involvement. The chapter also discusses the value and benefits of youth participation.

Chapter 3 includes a discussion on collaborating with individuals, groups, organizations, and community leaders, and others who are committed to the same causes.

Chapter 4 describes a process for assessing the needs of youth and determining the message, audience, and method for effective advocacy.

Chapter 5 offers ideas for the involvement of young people in the parish and within the community at large. The chapter also identifies both the legally permissible and the legally prohibited lobbying and influencing activities with which nonprofit organizations are confronted.

Chapter 6 provides a fully developed two-hour training session on the component of advocacy. The training can be utilized in various settings and with a variety of people.

Finally, the *Appendix* includes additional material for advocacy work within the political arena, including helpful hints for attending public meetings; details on how to contact local, state, and national legislators; and tools for political advocacy.

Each of us knows that when the voice of youth is engaged in churches, communities, schools, and organizations, young people grow more capable. The ultimate impact of advocacy is both simple and profound: it engages a large number of young people to lead successful efforts for positive community and systemic change. We hope this book will help you clarify your own beliefs about young people so that you too can become a champion of youth.

1

What Is Advocacy?

Have you ever found yourself speaking up for a young person who has been misunderstood by others? Have you found yourself speaking on behalf of young people to parents or to parish leadership? Perhaps you have written a letter to civic leaders or attended community meetings in support of young people. Have you organized young people to speak at a town council or a board of education meeting on behalf of an issue that concerns them? If you answered yes to any of the preceding questions, then you can call yourself an advocate for youth.

Advocates develop their vision and ideas and put their words into action to create positive change that improves young people's lives. Sometimes advocates speak on behalf of youth. At other times, advocates seek allies within leadership structures who will champion youth causes. Or advocates may seek opportunities for youth to speak out for themselves. Anyone can be an advocate—the only requirement is to actively support a cause that benefits youth. Advocates for youth can include nonprofit organizations, businesses, government officials, researchers, teachers, parents, young people, churches, and the community at large. We advocate for youth when we speak for them and when we give them opportunities to speak for themselves. We advocate for young people when we

- respect and value their opinions
- appreciate their energy and insights
- work with them, and sometimes for them
- let go of the role of leader in order to share power and responsibilities with them

- assess personally held stereotypes, judgments, and preconceptions of them
- provide them with the information, training, and support they need to succeed
- refrain from blaming all young people for the actions of one or a few
- schedule meetings to be held at times when they can participate
- plan for interactive activities that break through tensions and age barriers
- plan meaningful and challenging opportunities for them to serve in the community
- offer moral support and encouragement to them
- support community organizations that involve young people in meaningful roles
- listen to them express their concerns and perspectives about community issues, and help them take action
- make sure they're at the table when a group of adults is holding a discussion about them
- connect with other adult allies
- talk with others about the importance of having a community vision for community youth development
- ask the question, "How does this affect young people?"

An advocate ensures that all members of society, including those in the Church, respect the dignity and rights of teenagers and their families.

Advocacy as a Ministry

In 1997, the United States Conference of Catholic Bishops approved *Renewing the Vision: A Framework for Catholic Youth Ministry* as a foundation for a holistic approach to the field of Catholic youth ministry. *Renewing the Vision* challenges parishes to be comprehensive in their approach to meet the needs of adolescents.

Renewing the Vision sets forth eight components of a comprehensive ministry with youth including advocacy, catechesis, community life, evangelization, justice and service, leadership development, pastoral care, and prayer and worship.

The ministry of advocacy challenges the communities of faith and society to consider how well the needs of young people are being met and how well young people are being integrated into the community. Advocacy happens when we help the parish as a whole and the community at large become more youth friendly, enlisting the community's commitment to welcome and value youth.

In addition to the eight components, *Renewing the Vision* provides Catholic youth ministry with three goals:

- *To empower young people to live as disciples of Jesus Christ in our world today* (p. 9).

This emphasis on discipleship is also reflected in the Vatican's *General Directory for Catechesis* (1998) and in the U.S. Catholic Bishops' *National Directory for Catechesis* (2005). These are the definitive reference books for the formation of catechists and for the preparation of catechetical materials. An important dimension of advocacy includes creating opportunities for the call to discipleship to be heard, the skills of discipleship to be learned, and the chance for discipleship to be lived.

- *To draw young people to responsible participation in the life, mission, and work of the Catholic faith community* (p. 11).

One of the major shifts in Catholic youth ministry over the years has been the emphasis on integrating young people more fully into the life of the faith community, rather than ministering to them as an age-segregated entity attached to the faith community. Of the three goals, this one provides a fertile environment for intentional advocacy.

- *To foster the total personal and spiritual growth of each young person* (p. 15).

Catholic youth ministry is holistic, providing for the emotional, relational, psychological, and faith growth of young people. Advocacy creates opportunities that foster this holistic development. Advocacy not only creates avenues for young people to access personal and spiritual growth, it also identifies avenues in which young people can find their voice.

Advocacy for youth means looking at all the leadership and decision-making groups in the parish, schools, community, organizations, and government agencies to see who can speak for youth among those leaders. Sometimes the youth ministry coordinator or ministry leaders and volunteers will be the advocate. In other cases, youth can be included in leadership groups and can speak on their own behalf.

Compared to other components of youth ministry in which youth are often gathered, most advocacy happens behind the scenes as leaders build relationships and promote collaboration. Advocacy for youth and their families demonstrates a commitment to stand with those who are most in need in our neighborhoods and in society. In *Renewing the Vision*, parishes are challenged to examine their policies, programs, and ministry initiatives to make sure youth are considered and included:

> The ministry of advocacy engages the Church to examine its priorities and practices to determine how well young people are integrated into the life, mission, and work of the Catholic community. (P. 27)

Therefore, the ministry of advocacy includes these practices:
- standing with and speaking on behalf of young people and their families on public issues that affect their lives, such as support for education, quality housing, employment opportunities, access to health care, safe neighborhoods, and the availability of meaningful community activities and services
- empowering young people by giving them a voice and calling them to responsibility and accountability around the issues that affect them and their future (This involves education, leadership training, skills building, and organization to mobilize young people for action.)
- developing partnerships and initiatives with leaders and concerned citizens from all sectors of the community to develop a shared vision and practical strategies for building a healthy community

(*Renewing the Vision*, pp. 27–28)

The ministry of advocacy looks at Church structures and practices to more fully integrate youth into the life of the Church, and also looks to the community at large to address societal ills that threaten the physical and emotional well-being of adolescents and families. The ministry of advocacy calls all people to stand with and for youth in the public arena (in favor of life, education, housing, employment, and other issues). It calls all to empower young people to speak for themselves on issues that affect them, and it calls ministry leaders to develop partnerships with others who will work for community-wide solutions that help put children and families first.

Dimensions of Advocacy—Intentional and Infused

The ministry of advocacy is not a single function. It cannot be defined with just one activity. Rather, the ministry of advocacy is a posture or a mind-set that calls all ministry leaders (and the entire community) to be "for" young people. The ministry of advocacy has two distinct dimensions. Advocacy can be either intentional (using proactive strategies) or infused (integrating a pro-youth stance into other activities).

Advocacy is intentional when individuals become the voice for youth or for youth ministry, and when the community speaks on behalf of all the young people. Advocacy is also an intentional activity when we enable young people to speak for themselves. Oftentimes young people are concerned about an issue and don't know what to do about it. As advocates we can enable young people to find their voice and help them use it to effect change. Simple examples include helping young people prepare remarks for a meeting, write a letter, or even get a ride to a meeting. Doing whatever it takes to help young people speak for themselves is a way to exercise an intentional form of advocacy.

Advocacy can also be infused or integrated into programs by speaking positively about today's youth and educating others about young people. The ministry of advocacy should be integrated into existing programs, such as leadership training for adults and youth, volunteer recruitment, and parent education.

Advocacy serves as a reminder to the community that young people are a gift to be shared, not a problem to be solved. This fundamental attitude is critical because it impacts how we "see" young people. If young people are a problem to be solved, then our education, social services, and juvenile justice systems respond to young people as a dilemma that needs a solution. However, if they are viewed as a gift to be shared, then these same systems embrace and foster young people's uniqueness and honor their contributions.

Ministry For, By, and With Young People

All those involved in ministry have the opportunity to be champions *for* young people by taking on their causes and positioning themselves to speak on behalf of, and in solidarity with, today's youth. Advocacy for young people is characterized by those times when adults speak up for the issues and concerns of young people, both in the faith community and in society. Such opportunities include speaking positively about young people at parish council meetings, school board meetings, and community meetings; writing letters on behalf of youth for the diocesan and secular press; and advocating for youth's concerns with Church and community officials.

The ministry of advocacy is *by* youth when young people speak for themselves and interact with structures that affect their lives. Examples of this type of advocacy include youth membership on parish councils and local school boards; youth testifying to the city, county, and state councils on issues that affect them; and letter-writing campaigns initiated by young people.

Advocacy *with* youth includes those initiatives where young people and adults partner together to speak on behalf of young people's concerns. In many parish, school, and community structures, adults have the opportunity to involve young people so that the young people's voices are heard and their issues are addressed, while adults provide them with support. We advocate with youth when we stand in solidarity with young people on issues. For example, when we organize rides for young people and accompany them when they speak to church or civic leaders, we are being advocates with youth. When we help youth prepare testimony or letters, or offer to speak alongside them on issues that affect their lives, we are being advocates with youth.

Developing a Context for Advocacy

The Scriptures

Catholics believe that through the Scriptures and Tradition, God is revealed to us. Advocacy has a long history in both Jewish and Christian traditions. Beginning with the Old Testament and continuing through to the New Testament, the Scriptures not only contain the history of a faithful people's evolving relationship with God, they also explain a developing moral code based in justice. Throughout the Old Testament, Yahweh was proclaimed as just—the just person preserves the peace and the wholeness of the community.

The Book of Proverbs is clear that we should be advocates for others:

> Speak out for those who cannot speak,
>> for the rights of all the destitute.
>
> Speak out, judge righteously,
>> defend the rights of the poor and needy.
>
> (31: 8–9)

Throughout the Old Testament and into the New Testament, there are many guidelines on how, and on whose behalf, one should advocate. The Scriptures not only call for us to take on the individual responsibility of advocating for those who have no voice but also give us the communal challenge to care for the voiceless and the powerless in our midst. In biblical times, the powerless were widows, orphans, and the oppressed. The communal call to act is the scriptural basis for the Church's teachings on social justice, and it is in this way that the components of advocacy and justice and service often become linked. There is a dimension of advocacy in all justice work, as justice is often an action resulting from advocacy.

Old Testament examples of God's call to be advocates for others abound. The following table gives just a few examples:

Exodus 22:20–24 and Deuteronomy 24:17–22	justice and mercy toward stranger, orphan, and widow
Exodus 22:25–27	mercy and kindness toward neighbor
Exodus 23:6–8 and Deuteronomy 1:16–17	judge fairly
Leviticus 19:9–18	love your neighbor as yourself
Psalm 9:7–12,18	God rules the world with justice.
Psalm 41:1–3	regard for the lowly and the poor
Psalm 68:5–6	God's care for the helpless and homeless
Proverbs 31:8–9	advocate for the voiceless
Micah 6:8	act justly, love tenderly, and walk humbly with God
Isaiah 61:1	bring Good News

The New Testament calls all followers of Jesus to love God and to serve one another. The Scriptures tell us that the early Christians became known as a caring, sharing, and open community that was sensitive to the poor and the outcasts. Their love for God, for one another, and for the oppressed was central to their reputation, and became a matter of public knowledge. From the beginning, Christian advocacy was expressed in terms of charity and compassion. The New Testament Scriptures are filled with teachings that equip us to be better people. The second chapter of Timothy tells us this:

> All scripture is inspired by God and is useful for teaching, for reproof, for correction, and for training in righteousness, so that everyone who belongs to God may be proficient, equipped for every good work. (3:16–17)

The following New Testament examples illustrate the integral relationship between our Christian beliefs and our need to advocate on behalf of others:

Matthew 6:25–34	to be first before God, serve others
Matthew 12:15–21	Do God's will.
Matthew 23:23–24	compassion and a sense of responsibility
Mark 9:33–37	do not neglect justice and mercy
Luke 6:20–26	the Beatitudes
Luke 15:1–7	Jesus associated with the outcasts of society.
Luke 24:49	Christ empowers us to continue his work.
Acts 2:32–34	true Christian community; possessions shared
Romans 12:10–18	make hospitality your special care, make friends with the poor
Galatians 3:28	radical equality

We can see, from just the few examples noted, that throughout the New Testament, Jesus instructs all his followers to reach out to the poor and the marginalized. In fact, he says the Reign of God depends on it. In the Gospel of Luke, Jesus defines the Reign of God with these words:

> The Spirit of the Lord is upon me,
>> because he has anointed me
>>> to bring good news to the poor.
>
> He has sent me to proclaim release to the captives
>> and recovery of sight to the blind,
>>> to let the oppressed go free,
>> to proclaim the year of the Lord's favor.
>
> (4:18–20)

Jesus promised his followers that he would send his Spirit (which was referred to in the Scriptures as *Advocatus*, or an Advocate). His Spirit would remain with them and help them lead the life to which he was calling them. Advocates for and with youth, at their best, are spirit-filled. They speak on behalf of youth, they proclaim the good news about young people in the world today, and they help youth find their voice to speak to the issues that affect them and work for change.

Advocates ask themselves, Who are the poor among us? Who is captive? (the addicted or those trapped in destructive relationships) Who among us is blind? (the unaware; those who do not know God) Who are the oppressed? (the ignored or forgotten in our midst) Advocates look for opportunities to bring Good News to the poor, the captives, the blind and the oppressed, and to work for justice for all.

Tradition

The Tradition of the Catholic Church consists of the beliefs and practices that have been handed down by the Apostles to the successors since the time of Jesus. Advocacy not only finds its roots in the Scriptures, it is at the very core of Church teachings, especially Catholic social teaching. The Church's social teaching is a rich treasure of wisdom about building a just society and living lives of holiness amidst the challenges of modern society. . . . Modern Catholic social teaching has been articulated through a tradition of papal, conciliar, and episcopal documents. . . . The depth and richness of this tradition can be understood best through a direct reading of these documents. . . . The Church teaches that we are one human family, and that our responsibilities to each other cross national, racial, economic, and ideological lines. All of Christ's followers are called to advocate on behalf of those less fortunate than ourselves. As advocates, we should have a strong connection to the following seven key principles of Catholic social teaching:

- **Life and Dignity of the Human Person.** The Catholic Church proclaims that human life is sacred and that the dignity of the human person is the foundation of a moral vision for society. Our belief in the sanctity of human life and the inherent dignity of the human person is the foundation of all the principles of our social teaching. We believe that every person is precious, that people are more important than things, and that the measure of every institution is whether it threatens or enhances the life and dignity of the human person.

- **Call to Family, Community, and Participation.** The person is not only sacred but is also social. How we organize our society—in economics and politics, in law and policy—directly affects human dignity and the capacity of individuals to grow in community. The family is the central social institution; it must be supported and strengthened, not undermined. We believe people have a right and a duty to participate in society, seeking together the common good and well-being of all, especially the poor and vulnerable.

- **Rights and Responsibilities.** The Catholic Tradition teaches that human dignity can be protected and a healthy community can be achieved only if human rights are protected and responsibilities are met. Therefore, every person has a fundamental right to life and a right to those things required for human decency. Corresponding to these rights are duties and responsibilities—to one another, to our families, and to the larger society.

- **Option for the Poor and Vulnerable.** A basic moral test is how our most vulnerable members are faring. In a society marred by deepening divisions between rich and poor, our tradition recalls the story of the Last Judgment (Mt 25:31–46) and instructs us to put the needs of the poor and vulnerable first.

- **The Dignity of Work and the Rights of Workers.** The economy must serve people, not the other way around. Work is more than a way to make a living; it is a form of continuing participation in God's creation. If the dignity of work is to be protected, then the basic rights of workers must be respected—the right to productive work, to decent and fair wages, to organize and join unions, to private property, and to economic initiative.

- **Solidarity.** We are our brothers' and sisters' keepers, wherever they live. We are one human family, whatever our national, racial, ethnic, economic, and ideological differences. Learning to practice the virtue of solidarity means learning that "loving our neighbor" has global dimensions in an interdependent world.

- **Care for God's Creation.** We show our respect for the Creator by our stewardship of creation. Care for the earth is not just an Earth Day slogan; it is a requirement of our faith. We are called to protect people and the planet, living our faith in relationship with all of God's creation. This environmental challenge has fundamental moral and ethical dimensions that cannot be ignored.

(The seven principles are from *Sharing Catholic Social Teaching*, by the United States Conference of Catholic Bishops, pages 4–6.)

Modern Catholic social teaching combines social analysis with Gospel judgment, and can serve as a blueprint for advocacy. When we see that people are not being treated with dignity, when people do not have the basics of life such as food and shelter, when people are denied education, or when resources are horded by some and not shared with others—we are called to action.

"The ministry of advocacy supports policies and programs that support and empower adolescents and their families and works to overcome poverty, provide decent jobs, and promote equal opportunity. In all advocacy efforts ministry leader must remember to focus on adolescents and families with the greatest need. This is the 'option for the poor' in action" (*Putting Children and Families First*, in *Renewing the Vision*, p. 27). Poor, vulnerable, and at-risk adolescents should have the first claim on common efforts.

Guiding Principles of Youth Advocacy

Invest in Youth

Ministry leaders must advocate for young people from all walks of life, from gang members to honor students, fostering recognition of the important role each young person plays in the faith community and in the community at large. The call to invest in youth is predicated on two beliefs. First, that young people are leaders of today, not just tomorrow. Second, that healthy young people cannot exist disconnected from their community and a healthy community cannot exist without meaningful contributions from its youth members. All young people should play a direct role in their own development, ensuring that the policies and institutions that impact young people and their communities are accountable to all members of society.

Respect Youth

Ministry leaders must meet young people where they are by respecting youth culture, life experiences, and community relationships. Advocates also demonstrate their respect for young people by creating an open and safe environment for young people to share personal frustrations and life experiences. Advocates often spend time walking the halls of local high schools and detention centers, meeting with guidance counselors, teachers, or probation officers. Advocates get to know young people's parents and extended family. Relationships with young people extend beyond weekly ministry meetings, trainings, or rallies and into neighborhoods where advocates can develop a strong knowledge of the community—the values, traditions, and daily struggles that shape young people's lives.

Include Education

Political education along with teaching the history of political and social movements are powerful tools for mobilizing, educating, and inspiring young people. Advocacy includes the study and discussion of race, class, gender, and sexual identity as a way to connect with young people. In an effort to better understand the conditions young people face, advocates encourage them to discuss their experiences and to recognize the individual and collective impact of systemic discrimination—racism, sexism, homophobia, nationalism (anti-immigrant sentiments), and so on.

Promote Youth-Adult Partnerships

Advocates work with young people, not for them. Respecting youth leadership is a precursor to providing young people with the skills to navigate their lives and engage in collective action. In the ministry of advocacy, adults encourage young people in the development and exercise of their own leadership. In addition, adults provide support, access to resources, and mechanisms for accountability. With adult guidance, young people assume control of and responsibility for their own individual and organizational decisions, both good and bad. In all instances, youth are able to express ideas, receive feedback, and reflect on and refine their ideas with peers and supportive adults.

The ministry of advocacy helps place young people behind the microphone at city council meetings, on parish commissions, and in door-to-door conversations with their neighbors as they work toward community change. Being present and active within the faith community and the community at large, youth demonstrate their capacity to function as community assets and achieve real improvements in the life of the community. As young people assume a more prominent role in parish ministry, there is potential for cascading influence; as young people assert their voices in public discourse, the needs of young people get incorporated into a broader community agenda. Advocacy helps to generate a respect for youth and their issues among parishioners, business owners, Church leaders, elected officials, policy makers, and key community leaders. The ultimate impact of advocacy is both simple and profound: the engagement of larger numbers of young people in leading successful efforts for positive community and systemic change.

Evaluating Your Advocacy Efforts

In all probability, you engage in many forms of advocacy in your ministerial setting. The following worksheets will give you an opportunity to reflect on the community's advocacy efforts.

Youth Ministry Inventory

Items A through H below list various roles in and aspects of youth ministry. After you have read through items A through H, move through the scoring grid on page 2. The grid pairs each item with every other one. Start with the first row of pairings. Look at each pairing and ask yourself this question: If this was the only choice and I had to choose between the two, which aspect of youth ministry would I choose as my ministry? Circle one letter in each pair.

A. *Advocacy:* youth commission, youth speaking opportunities, young people as representatives on the parish council, youth on community boards, public relations and communications about youth

B. *Catechesis:* faith development, religious education, Bible study, faith sharing groups, retreats, and sacramental preparation

C. *Community Life:* recreation, social events, coaching, hospitality, outdoor experiences, scouting, discussion leaders, chaperones, and activity planners

D. *Evangelization:* public witness, outreach strategies, proclamation, faith sharing groups, invitation, missions, and revivals

E. *Justice and Service:* service projects, nursing home and institution visitation, soup kitchens, hotlines, justice issues, peace education study groups, clown ministry, work camps

F. *Leadership Development:* activities that call forth, affirm, and empower adults and youth in youth ministry, training programs, support systems

G. *Pastoral Care:* asset building, compassionate presence during grief or loss, crisis intervention, parent education, education on risk issues, support groups, referrals, networks with other agencies

H. *Prayer and Worship:* youth liturgies, developing prayer experiences, music ministry, lectors, Eucharistic ministers, youth choirs or band

Resource 1–A: Permission to reproduce is granted. © 2007 by Saint Mary's Press.

Youth Ministry Inventory, page 2

Scoring Grid:

A or B	A or C	A or D	A or E	A or F	A or G	A or H
B or C	B or D	B or E	B or F	B or G	B or H	
C or D	C or E	C or F	C or G	C or H		
D or E	D or F	D or G	D or H			
E or F	E or G	E or H				
F or G	F or H					
G or H						

Count the number of times each letter is circled. The letters you circled the most indicate your priority interests in youth ministry. Record the number below:

A _____   B _____   C _____   D _____   E _____
F _____   G _____   H _____

For Reflection and Discussion

These scorings may affirm youth ministry programming when the team has energy and interest in a variety of ministry components. It may challenge the current youth ministry programming if the team finds that gifts and interests are narrowly focused. This exercise reminds us that advocacy must be an intentional activity if youth ministry is to be comprehensive. Finish these sentence starters:

I tend to emphasize _____

The youth ministry team tends to emphasize _____

The components that need strengthening are _____

Practical implications include _____

Two Dimensions of Advocacy

Advocacy is both an intentional activity and an infused activity. Spend some time assessing the parish's strategies, in terms of intentional and infused activities on behalf of youth. List examples from your parish or ministry setting.

Advocacy is an intentional activity.	
We speak for young people and/or for youth ministry.	
We enable youth to speak for themselves.	
The community speaks on behalf of all our young people.	
Advocacy is an infused activity.	
Leadership training for adults	
Leadership training for youth	
Recruiting volunteers	
Parent education	
Pastoral care	
Fostering positive youth development	
Other?	

Resource 1–B: Permission to reproduce is granted. © 2007 by Saint Mary's Press.

For Reflection and Discussion

What do the results of this worksheet tell you about the parish's practice of intentional and infused advocacy efforts?

What places (programs) are well balanced?

What places (programs) need improvement?

2

Advocacy: Youth Participation

Some people challenge the notion that young people possess the knowledge and wisdom necessary to be involved in complex projects or issues. Yet each of us can likely think back to our own childhoods and remember activities where we as young people organized ourselves successfully—without adult help. Consider these stories:

- Seventeen-year-old Susan Sparrow of Salt Lake City mobilized a group of twenty peers at her high school to lobby state legislators. They expressed their outrage that women in Utah earn only sixty-six cents for every dollar a man makes. On one of many visits to the statehouse during their three-month campaign, they passed out cookies. Some were large, and others were thirty-four percent smaller, with messages such as "Aren't we worth it? Vote yes on HB 81." The result was passage of a new law called the Compensation Pay Study, which will collect payment data by gender—an important step in addressing pay inequity.
- Compelling testimony by young people, based on their personal experiences of discrimination, convinced wary Massachusetts legislators to pass a landmark Gay and Lesbian Student Rights law. The students, with the support of the lieutenant governor, spoke at hearings, met with individual lawmakers, organized a massive letter-writing campaign, and held rallies and candlelight vigils that raised public support for a law that aims to "provide all students with a safe and supportive public education."
- Students attending Baltimore public schools formed a group called Critical Exposure and took more than one thousand photographs

documenting the lack of funding for urban schools. Fifty of the pictures were selected for exhibits held in the city and at the Maryland General Assembly. Due in part to this very visual advocacy campaign, legislators decided to increase spending for school facilities by $100 million.

- Allie Young of Pinellas County in Florida recognized that there needs to be more education and visibility around the issue of eating disorders because of her own battle with such illnesses. She formed Helping Hands, a support group at her school for teenagers coping with anorexia nervosa. Her advocacy efforts include a campaign to raise awareness of the need for every county in the state to provide comprehensive services and treatment geared for those suffering from this life-threatening disease, especially those unable to pay for expensive hospitalization.
- Seventeen-year-old runaway Janna Koschene from Colorado testified at a congressional committee hearing and presented a vivid account of sleeping in cars and overnight shelters. She gave detailed recommendations based on positive experiences she had with a daytime drop-in center in Denver. Following her testimony, at a time of budget cuts, Congress slightly increased the level of federal funding for crisis shelters and other community-based youth centers.
- In Leesburg, Virginia, several 14- and 15-year-olds were angry that in-line skaters and skateboarders were banned from using sidewalks, parking lots and just about every other stretch of pavement. The boys voiced their complaint to their town council, asking for someplace to skate. Three of the teenagers were selected to serve on a parks committee, and they collaborated with architects and others to design a skating facility.

As we know, young people who cry out "that's not fair" at home and at school are apt to be moved to action when they see a similar unfairness and injustice in the world around them. This focus on fairness often calls young people to organize themselves in a variety of ways, including the examples noted above.

Ask a young person about their community and you will hear perceptive insights and clear ideas about ways to improve it. Ask a few more questions and you may find deep passion for equity and a desire to make the world better.

Too frequently, adults forget to ask for involvement from young people when they are working on youth advocacy efforts. When adults write off youth as apathetic and disengaged, they miss out on some of the richest resources in their community. Just as significant, young people miss out on a chance to make a real difference, build their own skills, and gain the confidence that comes when others value their work.

Youth participation means involving young people in responsible, challenging activities that meet real needs and allowing them the opportunity for education, action, and decision making. The effect is felt beyond the young people themselves. More simply put, youth participation is the process of sharing decisions that affect a young person's life and the life of the community in which that young person lives. Through their participation, young people can take their frustration with the status quo and channel that energy to create social change. Driven by a desire to bring about change, they are ready and willing to take on leadership roles—and to develop the skills to do the job well. Organizations that capitalize on this interest can help young people develop new skills, confidence, and goals through the experience.

The participation of young people gives adults a chance to see them in action. It shows those around them that when given a proper forum, today's young people are full of ideas and energy to make positive change in their communities, schools, and families. The adults and youth who participate in partnership activities are not the only beneficiaries of increased youth involvement in the programs and issues that affect them—the programs benefit as well. Involving youth in the issues that affect them has the following benefits:

- Fresh ideas, unshackled by *the way things have always been done*
- New perspectives on decision making, including more relevant information about young people's needs and interests

- Candid responses about existing services
- More effective outreach that provides important information peer to peer
- Additional human resources as youth and adults share responsibility
- Greater acceptance of messages, services, and decisions because youth were involved in shaping them
- Increased synergy from partnering youth's energy and enthusiasm with adults' professional skills and experience
- Enhanced credibility of the organization to both youth and advocates

(The preceding bullet points were taken from the Advocates for Youth Web site.)

Studies show that when the voice of youth is engaged in churches, communities, schools, and organizations, young people grow more capable. They enhance their academic skills with "real world" experience. They learn the skills to become leaders and citizens, and they learn the importance of helping and working for (and with) others. Research shows that when young people participate in positive social relationships and activities with adults, the following results are seen: a decrease in risky behavior, stronger communication skills and leadership experience, higher status and stature in the community, improved competencies, and increased self-esteem. Thankfully, more adults are recognizing that the long tradition of making decisions for youth without involving them has failed.

Adults and Youth as Allies

Adult and youth partnerships are joint efforts in which both age-groups are working together to establish and achieve common goals. A partnership implies that both parties share equal power and control in deciding what gets done, who does what, and how they do it. True youth-adult partnership requires more than bringing an intergenerational mix of people into a room. Adults must give up the control and leadership that they often view as their right. Young people must give up any distrust of adults. The process can be slow and difficult, but the results are phenomenal. Young people can partner with adults to serve on an organization's board of directors (or parish council); they can team up with adults to perform needs assessments, conduct voter registrations, do community service; or they can form youth councils to help youth identify ways they can participate in civic governance. Partnerships provide an approach for youth and adults who want youth to do the following:

- Develop more mature social skills, group processing skills, communication skills, and the ability to more competently resolve conflict
- Work in collaboration rather than competition, where every individual's contribution is valued
- Express themselves verbally, physically, and creatively in nongraded, nonjudgmental, purposeful settings
- Learn how to work at tasks using their minds, bodies, materials, and tools
- Have opportunities to both define the problems they deem worthy of attention and use their creative and intellectual abilities to address them
- Meet and get to know people who serve as inspiring and accessible role models
- Gain the ability and motivation to think critically, solve problems creatively, and conduct independent study
- Have a sense of purpose and a belief in a bright future
- Act independently and feel a sense of control over their environment
- Be able to see alternative solutions and attempt to apply those solutions to both cognitive and social problems
- Be aware of the structures of oppression and be able to create strategies for overcoming them
- Take the initiative to seek outside resources and sources of support

Attitudes Regarding Youth Participation

All across the nation, there is increasing recognition of the capacity of young people to be involved in the planning, implementation, and evaluation of projects and programs relevant to their needs and issues. But engaging young people as partners in program development often places adults in unfamiliar and even uncomfortable positions. The way adults have interacted with young people over the course of their lifetimes has often established patterns of behavior that are extremely difficult to modify. As a result, many adults say or do things, sometimes unintentionally, that make being a true partner with young people extremely difficult to achieve. Such behavior and mind-set must be changed in order for true youth-adult partnerships to take place.

In *Creating Youth-Adult Partnerships: Training Curricula for Youth, Adults, and Youth-Adult Teams,* Bill Lofquist developed the Spectrum of Attitudes theory and identified three different styles adults can use when interacting with young people. The following descriptions are adapted from Lofquist's three styles.

Style 1: Ministry to Youth

Adults who exhibit the "ministry to youth" style often believe adults know what is best. They rely on adult wisdom and can often forget that young people have their own opinions to contribute. These adults, although well-intentioned, feel the need to protect young people from suffering the potential consequences of mistakes and failure. This style can also be the result of an adult who wants an excellent program and isn't sure the youth will do a good job, isn't sure the young people will follow through, or just finds it easier and faster to plan things themselves. Adults who operate with the "ministry to youth" style seldom permit more than token youth participation.

An example of this style is the youth ministry leader who takes a youth concern to the pastoral council rather than enabling youth to present the issue themselves. Another example might be an adult writing a letter to an elected official about an issue pertinent to youth and using a young person's name and signature for impact, rather than having the young person actually write the letter.

Style 2: Ministry for Youth

Adults exhibiting the "ministry for youth" style often believe that adults should assist youth in adapting to adult society, and they welcome young people's participation in making decisions because they think it will be good preparation for adulthood. These adults sometimes delegate to young people small responsibilities, where the young person can watch adult decision-makers in action; however, they do not expect the young person to be a fully invested participant. For example, an adult might invite one young person to join the parish council that is otherwise comprised solely of adults. Often, in such a setting, a young person's voice is seldom raised and rarely heard. The same is true of some civic community organizations that invite young people to attend and watch, but may not expect the young person to genuinely contribute. These invitations would be improved by inviting more young people to the table, ensuring that the young people are fully trained for the tasks and perhaps mentored by an adult committee member.

Style 3: Ministry with and by Youth

Adults who have the "ministry with and by youth" attitude encourage young people to fully participate. They respect young people and believe that young people have significant contributions to make *now*. Further, they firmly believe that youth participation is critical to a program's or a cause's success. These adults not only accept youth having an equal voice in decisions—they encourage it. They recognize that youth have abilities, strengths, and experience to contribute. Adults who have this style are as comfortable working with youth as with adults, and they enjoy an environment that includes both. Adults who see youth as partners believe that genuine participation by young people enriches adults, just as adult participation enriches youth, and that a mutually respectful relationship recognizes the strengths that each group offers. This style shows up in a parish setting in the fostering of youths' responsibly participating in parish projects with equal responsibility for planning, problem solving, and decision making. Adults working from this style see youth as the young Church of today and the young citizens of today.

Levels of Youth Participation

In studying the issue of youth participation globally, researcher Roger Hart acknowledged that youth participation does occur in different degrees around the world, but can often be exploitative or frivolous. To illustrate his findings, Hart developed the Youth Ladder of Participation as a beginning point for thinking about youth participation in projects and issues. His descriptions of the various rungs of the ladder remind us that education, initiative, and investment are essential for young people to meaningfully participate in our programs. Hart defines successful youth participation as their sharing in decision making and collaborating with adults who can serve as resources and mentors for youth. The ladder analogy describes a steady progression of meaningful and shared decision making between adults and youth as young people gain more competence and confidence. Following is a description of each rung on Hart's Ladder.

Manipulation is the title of the lowest rung on the ladder. Manipulation occurs when adults involve young people to promote a cause they feel strongly about but do not help young people understand the cause. An example is when adults ask young people to carry political placards about school reform, but the young people know nothing about the issue they are "promoting." Another example is when adults ask young people for input regarding youth programming, and then the adults collect the research, analyze the results, and create and announce the programming without ever checking their assumptions or discussing their conclusions with young people. Oftentimes, adults use this approach simply because they are not aware that young people are capable of doing more or of fully understanding the issue at hand.

Decoration is the second rung of the ladder and can happen when the role of youth is geared toward prompting an emotional response from the audience. For example, decoration occurs when adults ask young people to show up at an event in a T-shirt promoting a cause, or to dance or perform at an event of which the youth have no real knowledge. Again, adults often choose this approach because they have concerns about the effective ways young people can be involved.

Tokenism is used here to describe those instances when youth appear to be involved or consulted in a process, but in fact the young people have little or no choice about the subject or the style of communication, and actually have very little opportunity to form their own opinions. For example, tokenism can happen when youth are asked to speak before conferences or groups of elected officials "on behalf of their peers," but no effort is made to educate the youth speakers more fully on the issue they are addressing, to help them formulate their own opinion on the subject, or to consult with peers to gather their opinions. As with the two previous rungs, adults often don't understand what young people can do.

The first three rungs of the ladder are actually considered, by both the young people and adults, as having little or no participation by youth. These levels of participation actually hold little purpose or meaning for those involved.

The top five rungs of the ladder describe levels where participation and learning are facilitated. Adults in the higher levels of the ladder exhibit more respect and confidence in the youth they are working with. Young people increasingly are given the authority to make decisions. An individual young person might achieve a higher level based on the progressive development of their participation. It is important to note that it is not necessary that young people always operate on the highest possible rungs of the ladder. Young people at different times might prefer to perform with varying degrees of participation or responsibility. The important principle here is one of choice: programs and causes that claim to have youth participation should be designed so that they maximize the opportunity for any young person to choose to participate at the highest level of their ability.

Assigned but informed, the fourth rung of the ladder, is the first rung considered to be participatory with youth. Hart puts forth important requirements for a project or issue to be labeled as truly participatory:
- The young people understand the intentions of the project or issue.
- The young people know who made the decisions concerning their participation and why.
- The young people have a meaningful (rather than "decorative") role.
- The young people volunteer for the project after the purpose is made clear to them.

In "assigned but informed," the level of the young people's participation is decided for them (assigned), the involved young people understand the aims of the project or issue, and the young people know who decided that they should be involved and why they are involved (informed). For example, the United Nations' World Summit on Youth involved youth in a meaningful way in a large and complex event that involved heads of state from around the globe. The organizers recruited and assigned a youth aide to each of the seventy-one world leaders. The young people were recruited from the home country of the leader they would serve. These young people were given training on the purpose, the process, and the desired outcomes of the Summit, so that they genuinely understood the importance of the gathering. They were also given an extensive orientation on the layout of the U.N. building. They understood their role as advisor, guide, and companion for each of the world leaders. The youth became experts on the U.N. building and the event, and had the important role of ensuring that the world leaders were at the right place at the right time. Although the youth were *assigned* as aides, they were *informed* so that the importance of their role was clear to them.

In **consulted and informed,** young people sometimes work as consultants for adults in a manner that has great integrity. The project may be designed and run by adults, but young people's opinions are taken seriously in the decision-making process. In 2003, as part of its philanthropic programs, Time Warner's Office of Corporate Responsibility created a youth advisory board to provide input on its new youth-focused grant-making strategies. The advisory group includes eight teens who consult with staff on grant-making, planning, and program development. At the Nickelodeon television network, programs are sometimes designed in consultation with young people. Low-cost versions of new TV programs are produced and critiqued by a panel of youth. The programs are then redesigned and again shown to the same panel of young people for their feedback. In this model, youth views are solicited, changes are made as a result of their feedback, and they see the final product their input created.

Adult-initiated shared decisions with youth is the sixth rung of the ladder. This rung offers true participation because young people are integral to the decision making, rather than simply consulted. Youth news publishing often involves the sixth rung of the ladder. Journalists can be brought in for advice and technical assistance, but the news stories are decided upon by the young people, and the news is written and illustrated by young people, thus allowing the true voice of young people to be heard and read.

Youth-initiated and directed, the seventh rung on the ladder, is infrequently seen. This is because it is often difficult for adults to let young people act on the strength of their own convictions without some sort of interference or involvement in making decisions. However, many young people are motivated to make a difference in world. One example of a youth-initiated and directed program is Happy Helpers for the Homeless, a program initiated and run by a group of twelve-year-olds who were moved to action on behalf of the homeless in Baltimore.

In the **youth-initiated, shared decisions with adults** model, adults are involved as facilitators. The adult role is to help young people reach their goals. Adults direct youth to resources, provide support in developing the necessary skills, and help youth evaluate their efforts. This model enhances participation on the part of young people and builds a sense of community ownership. It also provides the adults with an opportunity to learn from the creativity and enthusiasm of young people. *Youth-initiated, shared decisions with adults* is the highest rung on the youth participation ladder.

Hart's Ladder of Participation shows *youth-initiated, shared decisions with adults* as the top form of young people's participation, followed immediately by *youth-initiated and directed*. This is a somewhat controversial issue for many people working with and around young people. Essentially, the debate centers around the question of which of these levels of participation is actually the most meaningful. Many believe that shared decision making is most beneficial to both young people and adults. Others believe that young people are most empowered when they are making decisions without the influence of adults. Most often this doesn't exclude adults but reduces their role to that of support.

Both arguments have merit; ultimately, it is up to each group to determine which form of decision making best fits with the group's needs.

A true partnership exists when each person has the opportunity to make suggestions and decisions and when everyone's contribution is recognized and valued. The same principle holds true with youth-adult partnerships. In youth-adult partnerships, adults see young people as full partners in influencing the programs, policies, and issues that affect young people.

When adults participate together with youth in meaningful projects, causes, committees, and activities, there is true respect and great energy. They will find commitment, passion, and excitement from everyone involved, regardless of age. Signs of success in youth and adult partnerships include enthusiasm, clarity and understanding of the project or issue by all members, commitment to the task, and a growth in membership. The following are some practical tips on creating adult-youth partnerships:

- Select adults and youth who are willing to engage in the mutuality of the process that adult-youth partnerships require. Each needs to see the other as bringing a unique and valuable perspective.

- Treat young people the same way you treat adults.
- Give youth and adults the opportunity to explore the gifts they each bring to the table. Hold sessions in which participants share their gifts and their hesitancy about engaging in the partnerships.
- Create a clear vision of what you hope the adult-youth partnership will accomplish.
- Be conscious of the times at which meetings are scheduled. Are they accessible in time and location for adults and youth?
- Allow youth to make significant and meaningful decisions; avoid tokenism.
- Allocate resources for youth.
- Allocate time for the opportunity to reflect on and evaluate the work.

So often adults see young people as participants sometime in the future — when they are older. However, young people have gifts, insights, and perspectives that are valuable today. Further, if we expect young people to grow to be involved citizens in the future, in both our faith communities and our civic communities, they need to be engaged at levels appropriate to their skills and interests.

Note: Resource 2–A, "Assessing Adults as Allies," can help you determine the behaviors you exhibit in your own interaction with young people and those areas you may want to improve. This tool will also help parishes evaluate their overall efforts and gain more youth participation.

Inventory of Adults' Attitudes and Behaviors Toward Young People

Select the level that best describes your own belief or approach regarding each statement, and place the number in the blank.

1	2	3	4	5	6	7	8	9
Never		Seldom		Sometimes		Often		Always

_____ 1. As an adult leader, I engage young people in program decisions when I think it will be a growth experience for them.

_____ 2. It is most appropriate for adults to determine what the programs for youth will be.

_____ 3. Young people have a vantage point that is valuable for evaluating the successes and failures of specific programs.

_____ 4. In our organizational decision making, adults should make the decisions.

_____ 5. I believe that allowing young people to participate in organizational roles can open valuable learning opportunities for them.

_____ 6. As an adult leader, I engage young people in making program decisions at the earliest opportunity.

_____ 7. Asking young people to review adult-determined program plans will communicate to the young people that adults respect them.

_____ 8. Adults are in the best position to evaluate the successes and failures of specific programs.

_____ 9. Youth participation can enhance and enrich the various management roles within our organization.

_____ 10. Fewer mistakes are made in carrying out a program for youth if adults perform the leadership roles themselves.

_____ 11. I believe that the experiences of young people give them a valuable perspective that can be useful in efforts to plan, operate, and evaluate the way the organization functions.

Resource 2–A: Permission to reproduce is granted. © 2007 by Saint Mary's Press.

Inventory of Adults Attitudes, page 2

_____ 12. Asking the opinions of young people will help them sharpen their thinking and observational skills.

_____ 13. Allowing young people to assume some leadership roles can help them develop skills for the future.

_____ 14. In our organizational decision making, adults and young people should make the decisions together.

_____ 15. I believe that allowing young people to participate in organizational decision making would mislead them into thinking they can influence matters that are beyond their control.

Inventory Scoring Instructions

Transfer the numbers given to each statement into the style box that is shaded for that statement. For example, if you put a four by the first statement, then put a four in the box under the Style 2 column. In statement two, the number would go in Style 1. Total the numbers at the bottom of each column. The one with the highest score is the one that best characterizes your attitude toward youth participation in your parish.

Statement	Style 1	Style 2	Style 3
1			
2			
3			
4			
5			
6			
7			
8			
9			
10			
11			
12			
13			
14			
15			
Total			

Here is a brief summary of Bill Lofquist's Three Styles or Attitudes of Adults.

Style 1: Ministry to Youth
Adults who exhibit the "ministry to youth" style often believe adults know what is best. They rely on adult wisdom and can often forget that young people have their own opinions to contribute. These adults, although well-intentioned, feel the need to protect young people from suffering the potential consequences of mistakes, or they fear the youth will fail. This style can also be the result of an adult who wants an excellent program and isn't sure the youth will do a good job, isn't sure the young people will follow through, or just finds it easier and faster to plan by themselves.

Style 2: Ministry for Youth
Adults exhibiting the "ministry for youth" style often believe adults should assist youth in adapting to adult society, and they welcome young people's participation in making decisions because they think it will be good preparation for adulthood. These adults sometimes delegate to young people small responsibilities, where they can watch adult decision-makers in action; however, they do not expect the young person to be a fully invested participant.

Style 3: Young People Viewed as Partners in Ministry (Ministry with and by Youth):
Adults who have the "ministry with and by youth" attitude encourage young people to fully participate. They respect young people and believe that young people have significant contributions to make *now*. Further, they firmly believe that youth participation is critical to a program's or a cause's success. These adults not only accept but also encourage youth to have an equal voice in decisions. Adults recognize that youth have abilities, strengths, and experience to contribute. Adults who adopt this style are as comfortable working with youth as with adults, and they enjoy an environment that includes both. Adults who see youth as partners believe

Inventory of Adults Attitudes, page 4

that genuine participation by young people enriches adults, just as adult participation enriches youth—and that a mutually respectful relationship recognizes the strengths that each offers.

(The inventory and scoring sheets are adapted from *Making It Work: A Guide to Successful Youth-Adult Partnerships*, produced through a joint partnership of the Texas Network of Youth Services and the Prevention and Early Intervention/Community Youth Development Division of the Texas Department of Protective and Regulatory Services, pages 17–18, and found at *www.tnoys.org/TNOYSServices/PromotingYouthDev/Youth%20Adult%20Partnerships%20Guide.pdf*, accessed January 18, 2007. Used with permission.

The three styles of adults are adapted from "The Spectrum of Attitudes: Building a Theory of Youth Development," by Bill Lofquist, in *New Designs for Youth Development*, 5[3], 3–6, Fall 1989. Used with permission.)

Assessing Adults as Allies

How would you assess your own present level in the following ways of working with young people? (Circle one number for each question.)

	Low				High
Truly respecting their ideas	1	2	3	4	5
Giving encouragement	1	2	3	4	5
Providing resources for activities	1	2	3	4	5
Listening carefully	1	2	3	4	5
Promoting active participation	1	2	3	4	5
Dealing with bureaucracies	1	2	3	4	5
Building community support	1	2	3	4	5
Encouraging critical thinking	1	2	3	4	5

Scoring
- Add the numbers circled and put the total here. _____ (The highest score is 40. The higher the score, the more committed you are to empowering young people as advocates.)
- Underline the items that need the most improvement.
- Circle an item you could start changing today.
- Compare your score with those of other adults and discuss the results.

(This inventory and scoring sheet is adapted from "Adults as Allies," by Barry Checkoway [Dearborn, MI: School of Social Work, University of Michigan, 2004].)

Resource 2–B: Permission to reproduce is granted. © 2007 by Saint Mary's Press.

3

Forging Collaborative Partnerships

The axiom that two heads are better than one really is true. By thinking, planning, and working together, individuals and groups can accomplish goals that neither could achieve alone. Many churches, schools, parents, human service agencies, nonprofit and volunteer organizations, businesses, and local governments are realizing that by working together they can more effectively design strategies that respond to local conditions affecting young people, and can use community resources more efficiently.

We all know that people joining together usually can accomplish more than one person acting alone is able to. As individuals unite in solidarity, they also realize that their individual problems have social causes and collective solutions. This kind of group solidarity does not diminish the importance of individual initiative, but rather recognizes the strength that comes from joining together. Launching collaborative partnerships on behalf of the young can be exciting for everyone involved. There is a sense that "we can conquer the issue at hand if we all come together."

Forging collaborations begins with seeking partners who are committed to the same cause that you are. There are many catalysts for such partnerships. Some begin when church or school leaders or local policymakers initiate collaboration. Others form when a community becomes aware of an urgent need for change or when funding becomes available to respond to conditions in the community.

Here are a few examples of coalitions that have produced positive results for young people:

- In Albuquerque, a coalition of youth and adults studied a proposal for armed guards in schools. They then used their findings to hold rallies and distribute petitions, thus convincing school officials to reject the proposal for armed guards.
- In Fairmont, West Virginia, parents and young people were concerned about students drinking and driving after proms, so they created a coalition of churches, the PTA, and the local SADD (Students Against Destructive Decisions) chapter to address the problem. The coalition met to discuss these concerns and jointly sponsored an alcohol-free after-prom party that lasted until dawn and included activities, food, and door prizes that were donated by local businesses.
- In both Rapid City, South Dakota, and Houma-Thibodaux, Louisiana, the Catholic dioceses teamed with other denominations and local civic organizations to conduct training on the Search Institute's positive asset building approach.
- The Archdiocese of Baltimore's Office of Youth Ministry joined with other diocesan departments and organizations to create a "Coalition of Concern" to develop collaborative efforts for responding to at-risk young people.
- The National Federation for Catholic Youth Ministry partnered with Boys and Girls Clubs of America to network diocesan offices of youth ministry with local chapters of the Boys and Girls Clubs.
- In Des Moines, a coalition collected school system data, held meetings with the superintendent, and successfully demanded that an attendance policy be changed.
- In the South Bronx, adult and youth evaluators gathered data on juvenile detention facilities and presented recommendations to police and school officials.
- The Native American Club of West Seattle High found the name and mascot of its sports team to be offensive. Partnering with the Seattle Young People's Project (SYPP), they held a news conference, published a letter in the daily newspaper, and conducted a rally. Ultimately the

board of education changed the policy; school teams, along with their mascots, no longer can be named in racially insensitive ways.
- The Multnomah Youth Commission (MYC) in Portland analyzed the coverage of youth in the region's largest daily newspaper, the *Oregonian*, and found that the few articles about youth that were printed pertained to crime or sports. The MYC began working with newspaper staff to improve youth coverage, and suggested the paper hire a youth-beat reporter to specifically cover youth issues and to create a weekly feature on youth. Both recommendations were adopted, and "The Zone" was created as a weekly feature.
- Youth Making A Change (YMAC) surveyed students and found depression was a widespread problem. YMAC calculated that it would cost $109 per pupil per year to provide a qualified mental health counselor in every high school. At first YMAC was not successful in convincing the San Francisco board of supervisors, but YMAC persisted and ultimately succeeded.
- A group of students at King City High School in California wanted the vending machines to offer snacks other than chips and candy bars. The group collaborated with the vice principal, other school administrators, and the snack company to find low-fat foods that could be sold in the machines. The group conducted a taste-test on campus so that the entire student body could vote on which snacks they preferred. As a result, vending machines at this school now are filled with pretzels, low-fat cereal bars, and other healthier snacks.
- The San Francisco Youth Commission consists of seventeen members between the ages of twelve and twenty-three, who review any legislation pertaining to young people.
- Parishes throughout the United States have recently forged collaborative partnerships with schools, parishes, and Catholic charities in Gulf Coast dioceses in order to provide ongoing assistance in the wake of hurricanes Katrina and Rita.

The participants in many of these coalitions reported results beyond the issues they were working on. They found themselves advocating for young people, challenging adult attitudes, and questioning discomforting practices. They also reported increased intergenerational interaction and a change in organizational culture.

How to Begin

If you are looking to create a partnership, begin by building on historically successful alliances in the community. If there are groups who are interested in the same issues and causes that you are, contact them and join their efforts—you do not have to act alone or reinvent the wheel. You can influence existing groups to adopt your cause as their own. You will also want to discover which local conditions will support or inhibit a collaborative effort. You can learn about a community's readiness for collaboration by talking with school administrators, parents, volunteer coordinators, religious leaders, city or county council members, and representatives of neighborhood and youth-serving organizations. You may want to consider the following questions:

- Which stakeholders have an interest in the partnership you are planning?
- Who might be willing to join the collaboration? Will the attitudes and culture of these individuals or groups support the partnership?
- Are potential partners willing to share their resources and capacities?
- How do the interests of each potential partner fit into the broader collaboration?

When you build partnerships, involve people and organizations that are seen as leaders in the community. Aligning yourself with people who already wield influence can strengthen the cause. The partnership should strive to foster mutual respect, understanding, and trust among the stakeholders.

As the partnership begins to take shape, make sure you are attracting appropriate participants to the collaborating table—and that they can work effectively once they get there. Some of those who are experienced in partnerships offer the following advice:

- Ensure a broad-based, inclusive partnership by seeking partners who represent a cross-section of the community: parents, principals, teachers, counselors and other school staff, cultural and religious leaders, health care and human services providers, business and political leaders, staff and administrators from community organizations, and representative student groups. Make sure partners reflect diverse perspectives, experiences, ages, cultures, and levels of authority.
- Secure a commitment to collaboration. You may want to ask partner organizations to designate representatives' names and responsibilities in writing; this makes it more likely the same people will be at the table every time the group meets.

Once all partners are in place, you are ready to establish a governing structure for the partnership. Take some planning time to consider the following questions:

- Will responsibility be shared equally, or will one partner take the lead?
- How will decisions be made among partners?

The answers to these questions will be shaped by the extent to which partners share goals, responsibility, and authority; the comprehensiveness of the partnership and its strategies; and the level of resources and policy support for the collaboration. The following guidelines might assist you as you build local partnerships to support your objectives:

- Each participant in the coalition must have a stake in the process and outcome.
- Be flexible, be open to compromise, and be willing to adapt. The will of the group may not always match your own preferences.
- Effective partnerships establish specific, concrete, limited, and attainable goals. Alliances and coalitions often have a limited lifetime to achieve a specific goal.
- Clearly define the roles and responsibilities for each of the stakeholders.
- Ensure open, frequent, and sustained communication so that each of the partners is fully informed.

- Determine how planning, meeting facilitation, decision making, and implementation will happen.
- Develop personal relationships.
- Articulate your shared vision.
- Ensure a commitment of the necessary time, energy, and resources from each partner at the outset.
- Demonstrate a high level of passion for your target objectives.

Find Common Ground

In many communities, the partners who join a collaborative group may not have worked together before, may not even know each other, or they may come from organizations with long histories of conflict and competition. And although diversity among partners gives multiple stakeholders a voice in the comprehensive partnership, it can also mean differences of opinion about issues and disagreement on the best strategies for addressing them. In order to shape a diverse group of individuals into a focused, trusting, and effective partnership, you will need to find common ground and develop a unified vision for success. Take time to help partners get to know each other and the participating individuals and agencies. As discussion develops around general issues affecting young people, encourage partners to exchange specific ideas, perceptions, and concerns. Discussion topics may include these:

- how local schools, agencies, and organizations operate
- what activities each partner conducts, and with whom
- how organizations are funded, how funds are allocated for activities, and how much is spent on each activity
- the effect of state and federal policies on agencies' ability to work with youth and families

Create a Shared Vision

As you explore perspectives within the group and find common ground, you can begin to shape a vision that will guide the partnership. Because a shared vision sets the tone and direction for strategies, it's worth investing time in formulating and reviewing the vision. This is an opportunity for all partners to think creatively about traditional strategies and to imagine innovative changes. Promote inclusion by soliciting ideas from all participants during the visioning process. Write down ideas as they emerge to validate the contributions of all participants. Use a variety of approaches to capture ideas. Use pictures, charts, diagrams, and color-coded lists to record participants' ideas.

Learning Opportunities

Collaborative partnerships often bring together individuals with very different knowledge bases, attitudes, and assumptions. Each partner possesses unique knowledge and skills that can benefit the others. As partners organize, plan strategies, and move forward, they create learning opportunities for themselves and each other. It is tempting to "just do it"—to assess, plan, and organize for action as quickly as possible in order to begin implementation. But it is essential to take the time to build knowledge and support if you want partners to reflect on the effort as they develop it and have a shared understanding of the work they are doing. This is the real work of a partnership: to build a community of learners by allowing different stakeholders to come to consensus and common understanding.

Collaborative partnerships work. Combining the efforts of like-minded people working toward a goal increases the energy and support for the issue. Partnerships provide support for us as advocates by putting us in touch with others who care about our causes. Partnerships are an important way that advocates call others to action on behalf of young people.

4

A Process for Advocacy

Decisions affecting children and youth are being made at levels far outside congregation or school boundaries. These levels include businesses, human services agencies, health care organizations, civic associations, governmental agencies, and others. It is hard to know what issues to advocate for and where to put our energies.

When a convenience store puts up a sign saying only two young people are allowed inside at one time, it is an example of a decision affecting children and youth that is made outside parish boundaries. When human services agencies cut funds and services for teenagers, when the government passes legislation designed to incarcerate mentally ill teens rather than provide treatment, or when civic associations say that youth are not allowed to skateboard on neighborhood streets—these are all examples of areas that may call for advocacy efforts.

Advocacy is not just about fighting for a cause; it includes developing a clear understanding of those with opposing views. In regard to the above example, we need to understand why young people are prohibited from skateboarding on neighborhood streets, because there might be a practical and legitimate reason for this city code. What appeared, in this example, to be a case of discrimination against young people really was a case of the city protecting itself against lawsuits from young people hurt while skateboarding. Yet if we look more deeply into the issue, we would see that young people and the city wanted a safe place to skateboard. Working with the opposing side, rather than against it, could produce much better results. Rather than just "winning for our side," the best advocacy efforts attempt to find solutions that address the concerns and needs of all involved. This requires good communication, understanding, listening, and negotiations all around. We need to center our efforts around finding clear resolutions that everyone can live with, when and if that is possible.

In order to be effective advocates for youth, ministry leaders may need to intentionally engage in a process of assessment that involves a step-by-step look at an issue. The following process can help to focus advocacy efforts.

Assessment: Analysis, Action, Reflection

A lasting solution needs to get to the root causes of a problem or issue. Problems and issues have many causes and many possible solutions. Advocacy strategies attempt to solve a problem or address an issue step-by-step by getting at its systemic causes and focusing on specific issues.

Analysis

Analysis involves exploring the origins and systemic causes of social and political problems. This includes seeking out those with opposing views in order to fully understand their perspective and rationale. Too often this is an aspect of advocacy that is overlooked or completely ignored. Oftentimes simple solutions can be found and determined by sitting down and talking with others who might think differently about a concern or an issue. This is why analysis *must always* include the seeking of information from "the opposing side."

An effective advocacy effort carefully takes stock of the advocacy resources that are already there to be built on. This includes past advocacy work that is related, alliances already in place, staff, and other people's capacity. In short, you don't start from scratch, you start from building on what you've got.

After taking stock of the advocacy resources you have, the next step is to identify the advocacy resources you need that aren't there yet. This means looking at alliances that need to be built and at capacities such as outreach, media, and research, which are crucial to any effort. What would be an effective way to begin to move the strategy forward? What are some potential short-term goals or projects that would bring the right people together, symbolize the larger work ahead, and create something achievable that lays the groundwork for the next step?

In many cases, advocacy helps young people unravel the personal and political, allowing them to understand their personal struggles in broader social and political contexts. Analysis builds skills such as researching, planning, critical thinking, strategy development, debate, consensus building, and discussion. Analysis encompasses broad community issues such as employment, housing, education, racism, and poverty, and can also involve issues that affect young people personally, such as sexism, ageism, and harassment due to sexual orientation.

However, until you are clear about the issues, it is difficult to move forward in the advocacy process. The following questions can help focus an analysis:

- *What is the situation* that calls for involvement? Be certain to conduct the necessary research to become informed on the pertinent issues. Know the challenges, obstacles, and past history of the situation.
- *Who are the people* who think differently from you? How do they approach the concern or issue? Are there ways to seek out compromise and simple resolution? Considering the opposing view may help put the issue into greater perspective, and may help you resolve it more quickly, allowing for a win-win solution.
- *What do you hope to accomplish* through your involvement? Any advocacy effort must begin with a sense of its goals. Remember that working with the opposing side (if possible) is always the best option. Among these goals some distinctions are important. What are the long-term goals and what are the short-term goals? What are the content goals (e.g., policy change) and what are the process goals (e.g., building community among participants)? These goals need to be defined at the start, in a way that can launch an effort, draw people to it, and sustain it over time. Are there ways to come to a solution for everyone involved

(not just your side)? If so, make this your primary goal. Are you looking to change an opinion, a policy, or a system? Are you hoping to change the faith community or the civic community? Or are you looking for changes from state or federal government?

Note: A common confusion in the development of advocacy goals is the difference between "goals" and "objectives." Objectives are specific actions—circulating petitions, writing letters, staging a protest—that are the building blocks of advocacy. A goal is something larger, and can be determined by asking these questions:

- *Whose voice needs to be heard?* (Is it the youth, youth advocate, parent, or other?) The same message has a very different impact depending on who communicates it. Who are the most credible messengers for different audiences? In some cases, these messengers are "experts" whose credibility is largely technical. In other cases, we need to engage the "authentic voices," those who can speak from personal experience. What do we need to do to equip these messengers, both in terms of information and increasing their comfort level as advocates? Sometimes when we are serving as advocates, it is an adult function where we speak up on behalf of young people. At other times advocacy means placing youth in situations where they speak to the issues themselves (and they may or may not need our help in preparing). Advocacy may include rallying other people, such as parents, teachers, counselors, or others, to speak on behalf of issues. And at times, we may want youth and adult voices to join in unison.
- *What is the message that needs to be heard?* Reaching different audiences requires crafting and framing a set of messages that will be persuasive. Although these messages must always be rooted in the same basic truth, they also need to be tailored differently to different audiences depending on what they are ready to hear. In most cases, advocacy messages will have two basic components: an appeal to what is right and an appeal to the audience's self-interest. It is important to assist young people to clearly state the message that needs to be conveyed, to formulate achievable goals, and to project their desired outcomes. The initial statement of the issue greatly affects the proposed solutions and

strategies that follow. Knowing what message to promote is essential, so take the time to craft the message so that it includes all that you hope to accomplish.

- *Identify who needs to hear the voices.* Who are the people and institutions you need to inform and involve? Spend time identifying an issue's stakeholders and the decision makers, and strategize on how to most effectively engage each of these audiences. Influencing others sometimes happens in big showy ways such as rallies and press conferences that engage the media. However, at other times, a less-public forum is more effective. Strategies such as formal testimony, a panel discussion, personal story telling, private conversations, phone calls, letters, and site visits may be more appropriate and effective. And the "voice" does not have to be a prepared testimony. A story can be told with a scrapbook of photos, a skit, poetry, or a tour. Try to assess how the audience will best hear about and be most favorable to the issue. You want your advocacy efforts to be the ones that will most effectively allow you to achieve your goals.

- *Are there other voices that can join together?* Sharpen your networking skills. Are there other individuals, groups, or organizations affected by the same issue? Often, building an alliance with others creates powerful mechanisms by which to educate and inform others, and to change systems.

Action

Action is the planning and implementation phase. This includes the traditional questions of who, what, when, where and how. There are many ways to deliver an advocacy message. The most effective ways vary from situation to situation. The key is to evaluate them and apply them appropriately, bringing them together into a winning mix.

Action may involve a collective, public activity that challenges decision makers. This should involve helping the opposing side see differently, with emphasis placed on working with them rather than against them. Here is where you point out the benefits of your ideas or approach. It can also involve a more private activity that aims for the same desired results. Action often begins by recruiting allies and members and engaging in community education. It includes a range of activities: speaking at parish council meetings, writing letters to officials, circulating petitions, displaying banners, and holding public demonstrations. Action helps young people build relationships, develop a sense of life purpose, and contribute to their community in meaningful ways. Action helps young people see their communities as places of possibility and change.

Reflection

Reflection is an important component of advocacy because it fosters personal, intellectual, and spiritual growth. Objectives need to be evaluated by revisiting each of the questions above; i.e., Are we aiming at the right audiences? Are we reaching them? And so on. It is important to be able to make mid-course corrections and to discard those elements of an objective that don't work once they are actually put into practice. Reflection can also deepen critical thinking skills as participants explore new solutions and cultivate new allies.

Reflection might include journaling, debriefing with peers about an issue or an experience, or discussing the effectiveness of a particular event. As an advocacy strategy, reflection yields insights and "lessons learned" from your experiences that can be applied to other areas of young people's lives.

More specifically, reflection yields at least three important outcomes. First, it fosters a sense of commitment. Young people come to realize their role in fostering change in their communities, and with this knowledge they gain a sense of civic responsibility. Over time this ability to make commitments translates into other areas of young people's lives—family, relationships, school, and career.

Second, reflection builds young people's identities at a critical developmental stage, fostering a sense of hope and of the power to effect change. New experiences and opportunities encourage young people to apply those characteristics in other areas of their lives.

Third, reflection helps young people heal from harmful social and personal experiences by fostering emotional and spiritual wellness. Through support groups, prayer services, group discussions, and gatherings, young people develop psychological, physical, emotional, and spiritual wellness.

Some Examples

The following three real illustrations serve as examples for this process. The first two are examples from parish life.

Example 1

Situation: Two teen leaders in a parish program expressed an interest in the parish hosting a "battle of the bands" to showcase local teen musical talent. The parish leadership had grave reservations about hosting a large gathering of young people on the parish property.

Voices: The two teen leaders needed the opportunity to explain the concept to parish leadership that it was to be an afternoon concert featuring seven youth bands from throughout the county. In addition, the parish leadership needed to hear the voice of the volunteer adult coordinator and two parents who were willing to support the event-planning team. The young people needed to hear the voice of the parish leadership and other parishioners in order to understand their concerns and reservations.

Message: Music is an important element of youth culture. Many bands write and perform music that has positive values and spiritual messages. Further, the young people wanted to host this event because they were proud of, and invested in, their faith community.

Who needs to hear the message: The parish leadership, especially the pastor, needed to hear the commitment of the teen planners and their dedication to responding to the reasonable concerns that were being expressed. (Equally important, the young people needed to understand why the parish had concerns about the events.)

Other voices: There was concern expressed from some parishioners that the parish had no experience with such events. There were also several parents who were very supportive of the idea because their teens were involved in music and had attended other band showcases.

Action: A meeting was convened between the parish leadership, the youth planning team, and the interested adults to identify the parish concerns and the event goals. Tentative approval was given, contingent on the team addressing various concerns. The planning team contacted other parish organizations for logistical support and assistance with event supervision. Subsequent meetings provided an opportunity for planning updates.

Reflection: At the evaluation meeting, the young people reviewed the parish concerns, how these concerns were addressed, and ways to improve the event in the future. In addition, parish leadership offered their own insights about the event, both pro and con. They further identified the importance of enlisting help from other parish organizations, and they acknowledged that the planning update meetings with parish leadership spurred the development of specific task timelines, leading to better accountability.

Example 2

Situation: A parish youth ministry team identified a need to involve young people more fully in liturgical roles. Several young people had expressed interest in liturgical ministries, but the parish was not accustomed to teenagers serving in roles other than altar-serving.

Voices: Young people themselves needed to be heard on this issue, and the voice of the youth ministry commission, advocating for young people's full participation, was important. The youth needed to hear the voice of the parish leadership (especially the pastor and liturgy coordinator) and other parishioners in order to understand those people's concerns and reservations.

Message: Because of their Baptism, youth are members of the community and have the right to participate in the liturgical ministries of the community. Likewise, there is a corresponding responsibility to be trained well for the ministries. Good liturgical training would assist young people in serving the liturgy as well as adults did.

Who needs to hear the message: The parish's pastor and director of liturgy needed to support this increased participation and visibility of youth. Parishioners needed to value and appreciate the gifts young people would bring to the liturgy. (Equally important, the young people needed to understand why there were concerns about them serving in this capacity.)

Other voices: The parish youth ministry coordinator and the leaders responsible for training lectors, Eucharistic ministers, and ushers needed to be heard. In addition, the parents of the young people who wanted to be involved in liturgical ministry were supportive of the cause.

Action: The parish youth ministry commission met with interested young people to help them articulate their desire for increased participation. The commission then facilitated meetings between the young people and the director of liturgy and the pastor. Once approval was achieved, the members of the commission accompanied the youth to training and served as mentors in their new roles.

Reflection: The young people and the youth ministry commission met following the liturgy training to review the process, their new roles, and the learning and insights. The young people identified the need to invite other young people to join them.

Example Three

Situation: In preparation for hosting the Super Bowl, city officials developed a plan to move homeless people and vagrants from the tourist areas and the stadium districts for the week preceding the game.

Voices: Local faith communities, youth and young adult ministry groups, and advocacy groups learned of the plan and were moved to action on behalf of the affected people. Others in the community had concerns about increased crime that might result if homeless people were moved to other areas of town.

Message: No one's dignity should be sacrificed for the city's public image, and a long-term concerted effort on behalf of homeless people was required.

Who needs to hear the message: City officials and representatives of the National Football League (NFL) needed to hear that citizens objected to the plan. (Equally important, the community needed to hear from city officials and the NFL on why they thought these efforts were necessary.)

Other voices: Media, other faith communities, and other advocacy groups coalesced around this issue.

Action: In response to the advocacy campaign highlighted in the media, a series of "Super Bowl parties" for the displaced homeless population were hosted in various faith and community centers, supported by funds from the city. Young people were active participants in hosting these parties. Further, public debate was initiated about the plight of homeless people in the city and the need for additional services.

Reflection: This advocacy coalition continues to meet to serve the needs of the homeless population in the city.

Advocacy will be most effective when we attend to the variables described above. These advocacy efforts were stronger because they involved an intentional planning process that enabled the stakeholders to clarify, articulate, and implement their vision. Advocacy certainly includes helping young people find their voice; but equally important, advocacy provides the practical support to enable young people to move from vision to reality.

Note: The following resource is designed to help develop a process for advocacy.

A Process for Advocacy

This worksheet can serve as a guide or an outline for your advocacy efforts. Take the time to fill in your answers to the following questions.

I. Analysis

- What is the situation?

- Who are the people who think differently than you do? How do they approach the concern or issue? Are there ways to seek out compromise and simple resolution?

- What do you hope to accomplish through your involvement? What are the long-term goals and what are the short-term goals? Remember that working with the opposing side (if possible) is always the best option.

- Whose voice needs to be heard? (Consider both sides of the issue.)

- What is the message that needs to be heard?

Resource 4–A: Permission to reproduce is granted. © 2007 by Saint Mary's Press.

A Process for Advocacy, page 2

- Who needs to hear the voices? (Whom are you trying to influence?) Who are the people and institutions you need to inform and involve?

- Are there other voices that can join together? Are there other individuals, groups, or organizations affected by the same issue?

II. Action

- Who will be involved in planning and implementation?

- What strategies will we employ?

- Who are the lead agents?

- What is the timeline?

III. Reflection

- What reflection/evaluation process will we use?

- When will the reflection process happen?

- Where will the reflection/evaluation take place?

- Who will plan and lead the process?

5

Advocacy: Practical Strategies

Often the role of the advocate is to connect youth with opportunities. Sometimes the role of the advocate is to propose and to encourage others to broaden their perspective about young people. In this chapter we will look at the primary dimensions of the life of the faith community and offer ideas for the involvement of young people in the wider community.

Involving Youth

When involving young people for the first time, it may be important to assess an organization's readiness and attitude toward youth involvement (see chapter 2). When an organization invites young people into further involvement, advocates want to make the transition as smooth as possible to help ensure success. In recruiting volunteers of any age, a defined role description is important, as is determining the skill level that is needed to successfully complete the task. It is also wise, when recruiting young people, to make sure they have the characteristics and motivation needed to be successful.

Orientation and training, inviting more than one young person to participate on committees, and providing experienced mentors for new roles may also ensure successful involvement of young people in their faith communities and in the community at large. Advocates can also remain in contact with young people to help process the experience, assist with motivation, and offer advice and support.

Advocacy Within the Faith Community

Pastoral Ministries

Every parish has a variety of pastoral ministries: visits to sick people, social-justice committees, prayer teams, communications committees, community life committees, and so forth. Among the ways to advocate on behalf of youth is to ensure that youth are integrated into already existing committees, activities, and events, rather than creating parallel structures in the youth and adult communities. This form of advocacy promotes the gifts of young people and allows their gifts to be shared with the wider community. It also adds an intergenerational component to ministry programming. For example, instead of youth planning their own mission trip or work-camp experience, ministry leaders can consider creating joint or intergenerational service and mission trips. Instead of youth serving in soup kitchens as a youth activity, ministry leaders should strive to have youth join the parish's social-concerns ministry.

A Real-Life Example

During Holy Week of 2006, our parish held a weeklong intergenerational outreach to the Diocese of Biloxi by providing relief work following Hurricane Katrina. Titled "The Katrina Project," the parish delegation included seventeen adults and ten teenagers. Within this group were six families. The Katrina Project was sponsored and advertised by the Assisi Youth Ministry Commission, and all the publicity highlighted its intergenerational dimension. The group members ranged from sixteen to seventy years of age.

When viewed through the lens of advocacy, the Katrina Project was an advocacy effort for young people in that it fully integrated them into a mini- faith community and utilized their gifts on behalf of families within the Biloxi diocese that were affected by the hurricane. Young people were assigned to work at sites based upon their gifts—not their age.

Further, it was an advocacy *for* young people in that the planning ensured that young people and adults shared leadership roles in leading evening reflections and prayer. Young people and adults were also given tasks for community living at the retreat house, whereby cooking, serving, and cleaning responsibilities were equally shared. Finally, an intergenerational group performed the stations of the cross for the entire retreat house and surrounding community on Good Friday.

The Katrina Project also involved an aspect of advocacy *for and with young people* when teens from a local Mississippi parish hosted our parish delegation for a supper and social. The coordinator of youth ministry advocated *for* the gifts of young people when she invited the parish teens to tell their own stories of living through and coping with the effects of Hurricane Katrina. Advocacy *with* young people took place when the stories of these young people profoundly affected the youth and adults of our parish.

The Katrina Project was an excellent example of young people's enthusiasm, passion, and insight. In fact, one of the attendees—a senior citizen—gathered the young people at the end of the week and said: "My friends thought I was crazy to travel to Mississippi with a group of teenagers. I can't wait to get home to tell them how wrong they were. You all were incredible. You worked hard, you made me feel welcomed, and I was so impressed with your depth of spirituality. You've given me hope for the future of the Church."

The dynamics of this intergenerational experience can be replicated in most parish pastoral ministry and community-building activities by integrating young people into existing parish ministries such as ministries at food pantries, social committees, new parishioner receptions, hospitality Sunday, serving meals to the poor, community cleanups, visits to the sick and elderly, involvement in the parish's blood drive, and prayer chains, just to name a few.

Leadership Ministries

True advocacy efforts provide the opportunity for young people to meet and interact with the leadership of the Church. Advocacy occurs when we create opportunities for young people to meet with the pastor to discuss faith, parish, and church issues. Arrange for meetings between young people and parish committees or organizations.

Most parishes have a representative structure, such as a parish or pastoral council. The ministry of advocacy can become concrete by including members who represent youth ministry (either young people or members of the youth ministry team, or both). Advocacy can also happen by advocating for just wages for youth ministry staff. Young people can speak to the parish council and parish committees on the impact of the youth program on their faith formation.

If young people are not currently involved in representative structures such as the parish or pastoral council, then advocates for youth can utilize young people in presenting regular (annual or semiannual) reports about the youth ministry programs. Furthermore, there are also times when special issues come before parish or pastoral councils or parish staffs in which the voice of young people should legitimately be heard. (In fact, young people may even bring these issues to the attention of the leadership structure.) Here are three examples of such times:

- when a pastoral or parish council is determining the design of a new building
- when parish or pastoral councils are considering hiring staff to expand the ministries of the parish
- when the pastor is hiring a coordinator of youth ministry or youth ministry leadership staff

Young people who have an interest in the functions of parish leadership ministries should not be excluded on the basis of their age. Young people should be encouraged to join planning committees for various parish ministries if they are interested.

Liturgical Ministries

Full, conscious, and active participation in the parish liturgical life, rather than token or segregated involvement, is integral to fostering the communal faith identity of young people. Ministry leaders must advocate for the participation of young people in all liturgical ministries. Young people need to be visible and present not only at regular Sunday liturgies but also during special feasts and holy days, including Holy Week.

Sunday worship can also be used to celebrate young people in general or to pray for special events in the lives of youth. Excellent ways to advocate for youth include special youth-focused Masses such as the annual World Youth Day Mass (celebrated on the thirtieth Sunday of Ordinary Time in the United States); a Mass that celebrates the beginning or the end of the religious education year; or a baccalaureate Mass honoring graduates. Including important youth events, such as exam times, prom season, the end of school, and so forth, in the Prayers of the Faithful not only invites adults to pray for youth but also draws young people into the liturgical experience.

Within the regular Sunday liturgy are unlimited opportunities to advocate on behalf of young people, their gifts, and their concerns. Here are a few ideas:

- Bless special things; for example, bless a departure of young people when they go off to work camp, retreats, or conferences; or bless their driver's licenses or car keys.
- Provide the opportunity for young people to address the congregation at, before, or after Mass to share their reflections about retreats, work camps, national conferences, international events, and so on.
- Recognize youth who have achieved recognition in the broader Church or community arena, such as being given diocesan or national leadership recognitions (provided by the National Federation for Catholic Youth Ministry), or religious recognition awards (from Girl Scouts, Boy Scouts, and Camp Fire) that focus on learning about their faith.
- Involve young people in liturgical roles: hospitality, ushering, lecturing, Eucharistic ministry, and music ministry.
- Include young people in developing special prayer experiences to commemorate a national or international issue or tragedy, such as Hurricane Katrina, the Southeast Asian tsunami, the war in Iraq, the AIDS epidemic, genocide, or poverty.

A Real-Life Example

Our own parish community has an active and talented adult choir. The parish's music ministry also includes a choir for grade school children. Recently, at the request of some teens, the parish's music ministry has expanded to include a youth choir and band that regularly leads Sunday liturgy at the parish and a teen band that performs at parish youth ministry programs. Another excellent sign that advocacy for young people is happening in the liturgical ministries at our parish was the inclusion of the children's choir, the teen choir, and the teen band in the recent choir showcase, which previously showcased only the adult choir.

Education and Faith Formation

The majority of parishes in this country divide faith-formation experiences by age-groups. Although this model ensures age appropriateness in the larger sense, by the time young people reach their teen years, their spiritual and faith-formation needs can become extremely broad. An emerging emphasis on intergenerational learning and whole community catechesis can also offer additional faith development opportunities for young people. Many teens are ready and willing to delve deeper into their faith, and should be given the option of participating in "adult" formation experiences such as parishwide Bible study and faith-sharing. Motivated teens will self-select those activities when they are ready, and should be invited to attend and plan such activities with, and for, the parish at large.

Here are just a few examples from our own parish of young people's involvement in education and faith-formation programs:

- Young people serve as peer ministers for Confirmation preparation and religious education programming.
- Young people serve as leaders in small faith-sharing activities such as *Renew* and *Disciples in Mission*.
- Young people serve as catechists or volunteers in the parish's religious education program.

- Young people serve as leaders or team members in adult faith-formation sessions.

Communications

Communicating with the parish at large is an important advocacy activity for anyone working in youth ministry. The savvy ministry leader can use several mechanisms to achieve that result. Bulletin boards that are visible, vibrant, and up-to-date can be an excellent way for the parish to be aware of what is happening with young people. If the parish has a Web site, it too can be used to promote the work and activities of youth. Promoting youth ministry and advocating for young people can happen via newsletters, bulletin announcements, mailings sent to families, parish registration packets, and other broader vehicles the parish uses to communicate with parishioners. Some parishes use their bulletin each week to highlight the activities of young people. Here are some ways to use communications as an advocacy tool:

- Create weekly or monthly parish bulletin or Web site updates on parish youth ministry activities.
- Develop annual or semiannual reports on youth ministry activities for the parish council.
- Create a video of youth ministry activities that can be shown to parishioners at various times of the year.
- Develop a DVD/CD on the youth ministry program, to be included in the welcome packet for newly registered parishioners. This presentation could also be uploaded onto the parish Web site.
- Collect e-mail addresses for youth and their families, and regularly update them on upcoming activities. E-mails can also be used both as a reporting mechanism on recent activities and as a way to recruit volunteers and services needed by the youth ministry program.
- Write articles for the diocesan and local newspapers and letters to the editor.

Parish Community Life

Youth should also be integrated into the life of the parish community. Young people should be featured when parishes are celebrating milestones such as anniversaries or new buildings. They should also be significantly involved at parish functions, fairs, and bazaars (and not just in setup and cleanup). Ministry leaders advocate for youth by planning activities that reach beyond the young people themselves. For example, our parish created a series of workshops for parents that deal with timely topics such as "The Internet—a Primer for Parents," "Fostering Self-Esteem," "Youth and Sexuality," "Fostering Communication," and "Developing Family Policies on Prom, Parties, and Beach Week."

Advocating for young people within the Church clearly responds to the second goal of the Bishop's *Renewing the Vision* document, which is to foster youth's responsible participation in the life, work, and mission of the faith community.

Advocacy with the Community at Large

Decisions affecting children and youth are being made beyond parish or school boundaries in such places as businesses, human-services agencies, health-care organizations, civic associations, governmental agencies, and others. As individuals, Catholics are called to ongoing participation in public life and to help shape public policies that reflect their values. Parishes and other Church organizations also participate in public life by applying Catholic social teaching to key issues facing their communities, the nation, and the world, and by speaking out on the moral and ethical dimensions of those issues:

> As a Church we need to provide strong moral leadership and stand up for adolescents, especially those who are voiceless and powerless in society. We call upon all ministry leaders and faith communities to use the resources of our faith community, the resources and talents of all our people, and the opportunities of this democracy

to shape a society more respectful of the life, dignity, and rights of adolescents and their families. (*Renewing the Vision*, p. 27)

Advocacy in the larger community is geared to improving the lives and participation of marginalized young people and families and forging broad alliances for reform across society. This type of advocacy is variously referred to as citizen-centered, transformative, people-centered, participatory, or social-justice advocacy.

Every community is different in its posture toward young people. Some communities use an assets approach and try to develop structures and ordinances that are designed to foster healthy adolescent development. Some communities base their approach to adolescents on a restrictive or punitive model. As advocates for and with youth, we can influence decision makers and opinion leaders to leverage financial resources, policy decisions, and media coverage in support of positive youth development. Whether we are advocating for young people or empowering young people to be their own advocates, the first step is to get involved.

Utilize the Media

Youth advocates must use every available tool to educate the public and policymakers about issues concerning young people. Media exposure and coverage is arguably the most powerful tool at your disposal. Consider the power of the media in your own life. The media exposes us to messages and calls to action, to suggestions and the latest items "we need." The media can be used to increase awareness of issues, support or oppose policies, and engage additional advocates. Access to such influence is too important to ignore. Contact the local media when you have

- relevant and interesting issues related to youth that are worth sharing
- compelling messages based on the nature of the problems faced by youth in your community
- a new commitment to engage in work that will improve the well-being of young people

Attend a Meeting

It is not always necessary to build something new in order to be an advocate. Advocacy sometimes takes the form of "just showing up." You (or the young people themselves) might attend a public forum or join a committee that is working on issues or projects that represent youth concerns at a community level. Researching an issue often points us to gatherings of like-minded people who are already mobilized and meeting to address an issue. For example, if you are concerned about drug or alcohol abuse in your community, you may want to attend a MADD or SADD meeting (Mother's Against Destructive Decisions or Students Against Destructive Decisions). If you are concerned about pending legislation, you can attend a public forum or hearing on the issue.

Establish or Join a Collaborative Partnership

Collaborative partnerships (also known as coalitions or alliances) are a combination of individuals, or groups of people, or factions working together for a specific purpose. (See chapter 3 of this book for a detailed discussion on forming collaborative partnerships.) We hear of coalitions on a national level when political parties temporarily band together in times of a national emergency such as a budget crisis or rebuilding after a natural disaster. Or religious factions might ban together to jointly support a cause such as pro-life. Locally, a concerned group of clergy, youth ministry leaders, pastors, PTAs, or politicians might join forces to work on a common cause for youth. For example, such a coalition might provide communitywide training in how to develop healthy youth and healthy communities. Or communities might organize for increased youth employment. Partnerships could collaborate on sponsoring Scout units or safe post-prom parties. Collaborative partnerships can provide powerful support for many advocacy endeavors.

The possibilities for communitywide advocacy are endless—here are a few examples (Remember that some efforts require more resources, time, and commitment than others.):

- Explore with city planners the need for additional youth recreational services such as after-school programs, a teen community center, midnight basketball leagues, and so on.
- Meet with local officials about making roads safer for young pedestrians and bicyclists by installing stop signs, speed bumps, traffic lights, sidewalks, bike lanes, and trails.
- Help keep your public library open longer by writing letters of support to your city or county council members and the news media.
- Lobby to get a student member with full voting rights on both your local school board and the state board of education.
- Help improve counseling services at school and in the community by starting a 24-hour teen hot line, a school-based health center, or a stress management program.
- Produce a pamphlet, video, or public service announcement that can add to what is taught in school about abstinence, sexually transmitted diseases, or other health issues.
- Develop a theatrical skit or play about sexual harassment, homophobia, or gender stereotypes, and perform it for community groups and political leaders.
- Contact your local police precinct or the police chief to discuss community policing and other programs intended to reduce truancy, drug abuse, graffiti, gangs, and so on.
- Train to be a peer mediator at a local school to help resolve conflicts, and share your ideas on how to improve the school district's violence prevention policies and programs.
- Create a teen court, where young people judge and sentence their peers who have pleaded guilty to shoplifting and other nonviolent offenses.
- Address racism and prejudice by forming a group that sponsors school or community events designed to stop discrimination and celebrate diversity.
- Launch a "Teens as Teachers" speakers' bureau on an issue you care about, such as eating disorders, child abuse prevention, rainforest preservation, and so on.

- Speak to school, religious, and youth groups about freedom of speech and about what happens when student newspapers, radio and TV programs, and so on, are censored.

Advocacy in the Political Arena

Although the Catholic Church often speaks to issues that are both moral and political, it directs its attention to the issues, not to political parties or candidates.

All activities of the Church (and its parishes, schools, and affiliated organizations) in the political arena must conform to the requirements of section 501(c)(3) of the Internal Revenue Code, which prohibits tax-exempt organizations from participating or intervening in political campaigns on behalf of, or in opposition to, any candidate for public office.

As a result, Church organizations, as well as individuals who are representatives of Church organizations, are prohibited from engaging in partisan political activities, including raising money for candidates or political parties, making or distributing statements favoring or opposing candidates or parties, running for elected office, or otherwise participating in political campaigns.

Church employees and officials, however—including clergy and religious acting in their individual capacity as private citizens—may participate freely in the political process, provided they are not acting as representatives of Church organizations or utilizing Church facilities or assets. At times it may be difficult to distinguish between activities undertaken as a private citizen and activities undertaken as a Church representative, and prudence should be exercised in that regard.

Permissible Activities

- endorsing or opposing legislation, including ballot referenda
- distributing bulletin inserts on moral issues and on the moral responsibilities of voters

- providing educational materials on public policy issues, but not on candidates
- arranging for groups to meet with their elected officials to advocate for or against legislation
- encouraging letter writing, phone calls, and other contacts with candidates and elected officials about issues
- inviting all candidates for public office to a Church-sponsored public forum, debate, or candidates' night
- conducting a nonpartisan voter registration drive on Church property
- distributing unbiased candidate questionnaires or voting records on a wide variety of issues

Prohibited Church Activities

- endorsing or opposing candidates for political office
- distributing bulletin inserts regarding specific candidates
- distributing or permitting distribution of partisan campaign literature under Church auspices or on Church property
- arranging for groups to work for a candidate for public office
- funding or financially supporting any candidate, political action committee, or political party
- inviting only selected candidates to address your Church-sponsored group, or permitting or hosting political meetings on Church property
- conducting voter registration that is slanted toward one party
- rating candidates numerically, or "favorably" and "unfavorably"
- sharing parish resources, including mailing lists, with political campaigns or parties

The lists serve as a summary of the principle "do's and don'ts" of political activity for tax-exempt organizations. More detailed information on the guidelines can be obtained from the United States Conference of Catholic Bishops.

Contacting Legislators

We are fortunate enough to live in a democratic society, where our elected representatives are available to respond to the concerns of citizens. Elected officials rely on interactions with the public for information and support. However, they are also faced with myriad opinions and large demands on their time, so a prepared advocate is an effective advocate. When contacting a legislator, you should be well-organized, professional, and productive.

If you are not sure who your elected officials are, you can check your local phone book, your public library, or you can conduct an Internet search.

Communicating faith-based concerns about public policy to elected officials—through a letter, e-mail, phone call, or visit—is an often underutilized but powerful means of witness. Taking the time to contact elected officials is consistently found to be one of the most influential ways to affect their position. One letter from a constituent to a member of Congress is considered to represent the views of one hundred people.

Note: The appendix includes additional materials for advocacy work within the political arena, including helpful hints for attending public meetings; details on how to contact local, state, and national legislators; and tools for political advocacy. See pages 91–98.

Ongoing Advocacy

Finally, it is important to consider friends, neighbors, and colleagues in advocacy efforts. They are often overlooked as potential resources, but they too can be a powerful force to alter public perceptions and create change. Be intentional about sharing your knowledge of and passion for young people. Tell your stories; broaden others' knowledge of young people by supplementing their experience with your own. Let your stories become their stories.

Many people not involved in political activity have no idea what to do to make their voices heard. Be an effective advocate, and help your friends, family, neighbors, and colleagues join you as you advocate for youth in these ways:

- Include your friends and family on personal and parish e-mail lists; invite them to attend meetings with you.
- Encourage them to share their stories with their elected officials.
- Be prepared to share contact information with others who want to join in your advocacy efforts.
- Encourage "letter-writing" parties (they avoid procrastination).
- And, finally, encourage your friends, family, neighbors and colleagues to continue to pray for young people and their families.

Although some of the facets of being a youth advocate take skill and experience, most of advocacy is a behavior. It is remembering to be a consistent champion for young people. So regardless of whether your focus is your family, faith community, neighborhood, community, country, or the world, you can conduct yourself in such a way that others know that you believe in and support today's younger generation.

6

Training for Advocacy

Training others for advocacy is just one of the many functions in which advocates might be involved. This chapter provides the basis for a training session on advocacy efforts to, with, by, and for youth. Though this session assumes an adult audience, it could easily be adapted for a mixed youth-adult group. Likewise, though described as a single parish session, this is also suitable for a multiparish session.

Objectives

- To describe the basic principles for advocacy
- To outline a five-step process for advocacy
- To identify practical strategies for advocacy in parish and community settings

Overview of Schedule

The time frame is based on a two-hour session. You may need to adjust the following recommended time frame to suit your audience. You might also consider dividing the schedule and conducting two one-hour sessions instead.
- Part One
    - Welcome, Introductions, Opening Prayer, Session Overview (20 minutes)

- Participant Reflection (10 minutes)
- Developing a Context for Advocacy (10 minutes)
- Dimensions of Advocacy (15 minutes)
* Break (10 minutes)
* Part Two
  - A Process for Advocacy (15 minutes)
  - Strategies for Advocacy (30 minutes)
  - Closure and Evaluation (5 minutes)
  - Closing Prayer (5 minutes)

Needed Supplies and Preparation

* Gather the following supplies:
  - name tags, one for each participant
  - markers
  - newsprint
  - refreshments
* Write the following statement on a sheet of newsprint:
  - Advocacy is a ministry that ensures that the Church and all of society are respectful and inclusive of the life, dignity, and rights of teenagers and their families.
* Write the following statements on a sheet of newsprint:
  - Something I believe about youth is . . .
  - My ministry most includes advocacy when . . .
  - The most challenging aspect of advocacy is . . .
  - The desired outcome of advocacy is . . .
* The training includes several mini-presentations you will need to prepare for, including the following:
  - A ten-minute presentation on the context and rationale for advocacy. You will want to review pages 15–21 in chapter 1 of this book in preparation for this presentation.
  - A ten-minute presentation describing advocacy as both an intentional and an infused activity. You will want to review pages 13–14 in chapter 1 while preparing for this presentation.

- A ten-minute presentation discussing a basic outline or process for developing advocacy strategies for, with, and by young people. You will want to review pages 54–59 in chapter 4 while preparing for this presentation.
- You may wish to create overhead transparencies or PowerPoint presentations highlighting the key points you will cover. You could also list these points on newsprint.
- As the participants arrive, ask them to sign in and to make a clearly visible name tag. (Name tags may not be necessary in a setting where the participants know one another well.) Invite them to help themselves to the refreshments you have provided.
- Place newsprint around the room, with one of the following areas of parish life listed at the top of each sheet: pastoral/social ministries; leadership ministries; liturgical ministries; education/faith-formation ministries; communications; and parish community life. Place a few markers near each sheet.

Procedure

Part One

1. Formally greet the participants and introduce yourself. Thank the participants for coming to this training and suggest that their presence is a sign of their commitment to advocacy for and with young people. Then ask each participant to introduce him- or herself, describe his or her role in the parish, and share one reason he or she has for coming to this session.

2. Invite the group to take a moment to be still and quiet. Then offer the opening prayer as follows:
- Let's pause a moment before we begin our session and recall that we are always in the presence of a God who loves us and calls us to be advocates for young people.

- Lord, in Proverbs 31:8–9, we are told to "speak out for those who cannot speak, for the rights of all the destitute. Speak out, judge righteously, and defend the poor and the needy." Bless those gathered here on behalf of the young Church. Give us the vision, the skills, and the courage to speak out for young people when necessary, to encourage the voice of young people when possible, and to open the ears of the community to the voice of youth where needed. This we ask in Jesus' name. Amen.

3. Explain that this training session has four objectives:
- to define advocacy as an intentional and infused activity
- to provide the basic context for advocacy, describing why advocacy is an important component of comprehensive youth ministry
- to outline a five-step process for advocacy, providing a simple construct for planning
- to identify practical strategies for advocacy in the parish and community, highlighting reasonable activities, approaches, and initiatives for advocating for, with, and by young people

4. Referring to the newsprint you created earlier, define advocacy as
- a ministry that ensures that the Church and all of society are respectful and inclusive of the life, dignity, and rights of teenagers and their families.

Then refer the participants to the four open-ended statements you noted on newsprint and posted earlier. Ask the participants to consider their responses for one minute, and then, in dyads or triads, to share their responses. Allow about five minutes for sharing.

Next solicit sample responses for each question from the participants so that the entire group can hear about the individual conversations. Again, allow another five minutes for sharing.

5. Offer the presentation on the context and rationale for advocacy you prepared before the session. Be sure to include these key points:
- The Old Testament calls the people in covenant with Yahweh to care for the poor, the orphans, and the widows. They are called to be good stewards of the land and live in peace with their neighbors. They are called to be advocates for others based on their belief in a just God.
- Throughout the New Testament, Jesus instructs all his followers to reach out to the poor and the marginalized. In fact, he says the Reign of God depends on it.
- Advocates ask themselves: Who are the poor among us? Who is captive (the addicted or those trapped in destructive relationships)? Who among us is blind (the unaware; those who do not know God)? Who are the oppressed (the ignored or forgotten in our midst)? Advocates look for opportunities to bring Good News to the poor, the captives, the blind, and the oppressed, and to work for justice for all.
- While on Earth, Jesus spoke out on behalf of the defenseless and the poor. He challenged humankind to continue his work and promised a helper, the Holy Spirit, to assist his followers in continuing his mission on earth (see John 14:26). When Jesus proclaims and promises the coming of the Holy Spirit, Jesus calls the Holy Spirit the "Paraclete," literally, "he who is called to one's side."

6. Confirm with the participants that the preceding is clear and makes sense to them before continuing.

7. Offer the presentation on advocacy as an intentional and infused activity in ministry, which you prepared before the session. Begin by making the first point as noted below:
- Advocacy is an intentional activity, first, when *we speak for young people* — being a voice for our youth and for youth ministry in those places, meetings, conversations, and decision-making processes where the voice of young people is not present.

Then ask the participants:
- What are some examples of where we might speak for young people?

List the responses on newsprint.

8. Continue with the presentation:
- Advocacy is also an intentional activity when we enable *young people to speak for themselves*—enabling young people to voice their opinions, concerns, and suggestions, especially about issues that affect them.

Then ask the participants:
- What are some examples of where we can enable young people to speak for themselves, to share their opinions, ideas, and concerns directly?

List the responses on newsprint.

9. Continue with the presentation:
- Finally, advocacy is an intentional activity when the *community speaks on behalf of all young people.* There are situations and issues that require the entire faith community to speak on behalf of young people—either to the larger Church or in the public arena.

Then ask the participants:
- What are some examples of when the faith community might speak on behalf of young people either to the larger Church or to the civic community?

List the responses on newsprint.

10. Conclude this section of the session by noting the following:
- In addition to being an intentional activity, advocacy is also an infused activity. Advocacy is infused when the activity, task, or action has a larger purpose than responding to young people, but the inclusion of young people benefits both the community and the young people.

- Advocacy as an infused activity includes those actions, decisions, or initiatives that enable youth to bring their gifts to the community, especially in ways not currently open to youth's participation.

Break

Part Two

1. Welcome the participants back and then offer a presentation on the steps (process) used in designing advocacy efforts. Begin with these points:
- Advocacy strategies attempt to solve a problem step-by-step by getting at its systemic causes and focusing on specific issues.
- The following process can help, regardless of whether advocacy is to take place at a parish or school, or on the state or national level.
- *Analysis* involves exploring the origins and systemic causes of social and political problems. Analysis entails transforming a problem into an issue and identifying parties responsible for bringing about desired changes. Analysis also involves taking the time to listen to the needs of other stakeholders.

Questions such as these can help guide ministry leaders in the process of analysis:
- What is the situation that calls for involvement?
- Whose voice needs to be heard? (Youth, youth advocate, parent, or other)
- What message needs to be heard? What goals need to be achieved through actions?
- Who needs to hear the voices?
- Are there other voices that can join together?

2. Ask the participants to name some situations in the faith community or in society that require advocacy on behalf of young people. List the participants' responses on newsprint. Then pick one issue to use as an example for the remainder of the presentation.

Then ask:
- Though we are discussing young people generally, are there any specific groups of young people or others whose voice needs to be heard around this issue?

Allow for some discussion if needed.

3. Continue to walk the participants through each of the questions noted in step 1 above, using the example you selected. Allow for discussion as needed. If time permits, you can choose another issue and go through the questions again.

4. Conclude by noting that two additional steps make up the identifying process for advocacy. They are as follows:
- *Action* involves a collective, public activity that addresses and sometimes confronts decision makers and pressures them to make a desired change. Action often begins by recruiting allies and members and engaging in community education. Action includes a range of activities, such as speaking at a parish council meeting, writing letters to officials, circulating petitions, displaying banners, and holding public demonstrations.
- *Reflection* is an important component of advocacy because it fosters personal, intellectual, and spiritual growth. Participants learn to evaluate their strategies, monitor their activities, and even gauge their own commitment to changing a problem. Reflection can also deepen critical thinking skills as participants explore new solutions and cultivate new allies. Reflection might include journaling, debriefing with peers about an issue or an experience, or discussing the effectiveness of a particular event.

5. Tell the participants that the final part of the session provides an opportunity for them to identify practical ways to advocate for and with young people in the parish setting. To set the stage for this activity, remind participants that we live in a media world where immediate, short, and pithy slogans and sound bites are the norm.

Ask the following questions, allowing for responses after each:
- What are some slogans, or sound bites, that corporations use in advertising or commercials? Some examples: "Just do it!" or "Be all that you can be!"
- Identify current sound bites about youth from society, media, government, education, or the Church. Examples: "Our kids are falling behind." "Youth are not interested in the Church." "They are going to drink anyway." "No child left behind."
- If we had to identify our own sound bite about young people, what might that be? For example, "Youth are a gift to be shared—not a problem to be solved."
- In terms of strategies for advocacy, where can our sound bite be used? For example, if your sound bite is "Youth—the young Church today," you can use this on a bulletin board, on your stationery, in the parish bulletin, or on a report to the parish council.

6. Tell the participants that in order to identify other practical strategies for advocacy in the parish, the group will review the areas of parish life that were placed on the newsprint lists throughout the room. Quickly review each area title and ask for examples of activities or organizations that belong in that arena. Some may fit in several areas, but it is not important where an activity or organization is placed—only that every aspect of parish life is included somewhere in the lists.

7. Ask the participants to divide into small groups of four to six people. Tell them that each group should begin at one of the newsprint lists and brainstorm for five minutes, listing possible intentional and infused advocacy activities in that area of parish life. For example, in the area of pastoral or social ministries, advocacy might include enabling young people to serve on various committees or councils. In the area of liturgical ministries, advocacy might include creating an intergenerational choir where all ages can share their musical gifts. (If you need additional examples, please refer to chapter 4.) After five minutes, groups should move to a different newsprint list and repeat the exercise.

Note: If the group is small, you can choose to have participants do this activity individually.

8. After ten minutes, ask the participants to take their seats and review the newsprint lists, one area at a time. You might wish to jot down the names of participants who seem to have a particular interest in an area of advocacy.

Note: If time allows, or you would like to extend the session, consider using a similar process to identify practical strategies for advocacy in the civic community. You could examine the following arenas: school systems, justice systems, businesses where youth work, parents, sports programs, social services, and entertainment.

9. Thank everyone for their participation and great ideas (and enthusiasm). Then conclude the session by asking them to share their responses to the following phrases:
- One insight or idea I had is . . .
- My biggest challenge is . . .
- One idea I'd like to try is . . .

Offer a few closing remarks, inviting any questions or comments from the group. Remind them that this training is a form of advocacy for young people because young people deserve the best possible ministers. Then invite everyone to bow their heads for the following closing prayer:
- Let's pause for prayer. Creator God, we thank you for the gifts, the passion, and the enthusiasm that young people bring to our Church. We thank you for the commitment, the concern, the support, and the care of those gathered here. Grant us the grace and perseverance to be advocates for the young Church. And grant us "the serenity to accept the things we cannot change; the courage to change the things we can; and the wisdom to know the difference." Amen.

Appendix

Helpful Hints for Attending Public Meetings

If you are concerned about pending legislation, you can attend a public forum or hearing on the issue. The following tips can help you and the young people you work with be more effective advocates for your cause:

- Show up early to receive handouts and reports and to adjust to any meeting room changes.
- Sign in so that your presence is recorded.
- If there is a chance to ask questions, be sure to identify yourself and the issue you represent.
- Sit in the front where you can be seen.
- Bring handouts or fact sheets for distribution.
- Use the time before or after the meeting to talk to hard-to-reach legislators or public officials.
- Bring a friend or colleague.
- Write a follow-up letter to the meeting organizers to express interest in the issue or to show support.

Tips for Communicating with Legislators

Personal meetings with policy makers are among the most powerful opportunities to make the case for issues relating to young people. Your effectiveness as an advocate might be enhanced if you consider the following tips when communicating with legislators.

Do's

- Identify who you are and whom you represent immediately on each contact. Legislators meet hundreds of people, and they can't remember everyone.
- Know the issues and the status of specific legislation. Refer to the legislation by number if you are lobbying.
- Know your legislator. Have some idea of her or his position on the issues, past votes on youth and family-friendly legislation, and legislative and personal interests. These can help you tailor your arguments.
- Be respectful. Disrespect will not win anyone over to your point of view. You have the best chance of reaching an audience by being courteous.
- Let your legislator know that you appreciate the job he or she is doing—especially if he or she has advocated a position that is important to you.
- Think of yourself as a consultant to a legislator. You have expertise on the issues young people face. Understand the subject matter around your issue, and be comfortable speaking and writing on the subject.
- Be brief, stay on point, and keep to the facts.
- Be reasonable and constructive. Be honest. Never lie. Acknowledge opposing arguments.
- Ask for support.
- Keep the door open for further discussion, even if you don't agree at this time.

Don'ts

- Don't back legislators into a corner.
- Don't overwhelm legislators with too much information or jargon.
- Don't get into lengthy arguments.
- Don't be afraid to say you don't know. (Rather, do offer to find out and send the information back.)
- Don't confront, threaten, pressure, or beg.

- Don't expect legislators to be specialists. Their schedules and the number of bills make them generalists.
- Don't ask the impossible . . . often.

You can contact elected officials through a scheduled meeting, a letter, an e-mail, or a fax. The following tips are designed to make your communications more effective.

Visiting an Elected Official

Visiting a legislator's office, either locally or in Washington, D.C., is the most effective way for a citizen to do advocacy with an elected official. Visits with elected officials or their staff provide an opportunity to build rapport face-to-face. Generally, elected officials are eager to hear the views of their constituents. However, their goals in a meeting may differ from yours. You will want her or him to act, or make a commitment to support your aims, whereas the official may be inclined to avoid controversy and balk at making a clear commitment to you. Expect ambiguity, but don't give up. The following tips can help your visit go more smoothly:

- *Schedule ahead.* To schedule a visit, write or call in advance. State the specific issue you wish to discuss. Mention a preferred date and length of the meeting and the number of people attending. Confirm the meeting in advance with a written letter.
- *Research.* Be prepared to appeal to his or her personal, professional, and legislative concerns. For starters, learn something about the district and the member's election record. How did he or she vote on other youth and family issues? on similar issues? What personal information may be useful? Talk to friends who may know the lawmaker and his or her interests. Use this information to develop a realistic sense of what you can expect to accomplish during the meeting.
- *Strategize.* If you are visiting as a group, you should meet in advance to identify the most important thing you want to convey. Keep the discussion to one message and one or two main points. Be specific about what you want the lawmaker to do. Repeat your message in as many

different ways as possible. Determine who will be the spokesperson for the group. Assign other roles as necessary.

- *Introduce yourself and your cause.* Have each person in the group introduce herself or himself, and whom you represent.
- *Lead with your own story.* Let the legislator know why this issue is important to you. Point to success stories and to programs that have generated productive citizens and saved taxpayer expenditures.
- *Be flexible.* Despite the fact that you may have an appointment, be flexible. Your appointment may be cut short or lengthened based on the legislator's schedule. Know how to get your point across in a hurry (two minutes) if you don't have the full amount of time you had planned for.
- *Ask questions.* Ask what his or her position is on the issue you represent. Ask if he or she is hearing from other opponents or supporters, and if so, what those people are saying. Ask what will influence his or her decision.
- *Be honest and respectful.* If the legislator asks you a question and you don't know the answer, it is alright to say you don't know the answer but would be happy to find it and get that information back to her or him. Be polite and respectful, but don't be afraid to disagree.
- *Leave materials.* You should always leave supporting materials, fact sheets, or position papers with a legislator. Leave your contact information as well.
- *Write a follow-up letter.* Write a letter to the legislator thanking him or her for his or her time, and restating your position and your understanding of any commitments that might have been made during the meeting.

Letter Writing

Letters are an excellent means to educate and persuade others to your cause. A letter of high quality can make a significant impact. The following tips are offered to make your letter writing more effective:

- *Write a personal letter.* It is much more effective than a form letter. Tell your own story about how the issue affects you, your family, or your community. Typewritten or neatly handwritten letters on personal stationery denote sincere grassroots interest. Form letters, postcards, or petitions do not receive the same attention.
- *Be brief.* The letter should be only one or two pages long and should focus on one subject. Discussing specific current legislation receives more attention than general observations. When possible, cite the bill number or legislation title. It might also be helpful to summarize the bill because hundreds of bills cross a legislator's desk in a year.
- *State your purpose.* Be clear about what you are asking your elected official to do.
- *Give your reasons.* Make the letter personal. Let the elected official know why you feel strongly, but try to offer positive solutions along with any criticism. Emotional outrage, condemnations, and threats are not likely to be effective.
- *Ask questions.* A well-stated question can express a viewpoint, and stimulate a response, far better than a form letter can.
- *Say "well done."* Thank your elected official when he or she votes the right way or takes a courageous stand. We should not forget that legislators appreciate encouragement, as we all do.
- *Identify yourself.* Make sure your return address is legible.

Note: Organizing a letter-writing campaign, so that an elected official receives a number of thoughtful and personalized letters on an issue, is an effective use of the letter-writing tool. Creativity, such as writing a hunger letter on a paper plate, underscores your message and makes the letter more noticeable. If people are less motivated to write their own letters, having one letter with many people signing on (with their names and addresses) is a second-choice option.

If you are not sure who your elected officials are, you can check your local phone book or public library or do a search on the Internet.

To write to a member of Congress, you should use the following addresses and salutations:

The Honorable _____
United States Senate
Washington, DC 20510
Dear Senator _____,

The Honorable _____
U.S. House of Representatives
Washington, DC 20515
Dear Congressman (Congresswoman) _____,

To write to a governor or state legislator:
The Honorable _____
State House, Room _____
Your State Capital, ZIP
Dear Representative/Senator/Governor _____,

The following suggestions and sample letter can give you an idea of an effective letter to an elected official.

In the first paragraph, describe who you are and the issue you are interested in discussing, for example:

> *I am a youth minister at Saint Pius Catholic Church. I am also a member of our regional social justice committee, which is composed of professional youth workers concerned about human dignity. I am writing today to ask for your support in raising the federal minimum wage.*

Use the second and subsequent paragraphs to communicate what you think. Use the facts you collected in your research, as well as personal experiences or stories, to amplify your main points, for example:

> *Nearly thirty-six million Americans live in poverty. Increasing the minimum wage to a living wage is a step in the right direction in America's ongoing march against poverty. The minimum wage has remained at $5.15 an hour since it*

was last raised in 1997. Yet, in today's world, the minimum wage for a mother who works full-time to support one young person falls $1,044 below the federal poverty line. Our parish has a large number of single mothers with children under eighteen who could better provide for their family's basic needs of food, clothing, shelter, health care, and education if they only had a slight increase in the minimum wage.

Close the correspondence, writing that you appreciate the official giving you his or her time and considering your thoughts. Restate your position, and request a response, for example:

Please support our workforce by raising the minimum wage. I appreciate your leadership on this issue, and I look forward to your response.

Phone Calls

Telephone calls are especially useful when time is short, such as when an important vote is scheduled. Phone calls also have impact when they immediately follow media coverage. In most cases you will not speak directly with an elected official; however, offices keep a "count" of constituent contacts, and this information is passed on and does have influence. The following tips can help make your call most effective:

- Prepare your remarks in advance. Focus on one topic.
- Identify yourself as a constituent.
- State exactly what you are calling about—an issue, a bill number, and so on.
- Be sure to write down the name of the person you spoke with and her or his contact information for future reference.
- Say what you want the official to do, such as vote against a bill or vote in favor of a budget item.
- Leave your name, address, and phone number.
- Be positive and avoid debate.

Note: Calling local offices of federal and state officials is okay, but calling their capitol office is more effective. For a state official, call the central switchboard at your state capitol and ask to be connected. Sometimes governors or state elected officials establish "hot lines" and invite callers to express their opinions on an issue. You can ask at your state capitol switchboard if an 800-number hot line exists.

Faxes and E-mail

Faxes and e-mail should follow the same outline as letters. Sending a fax can be especially helpful when a vote is imminent and there is not enough time for a letter. It is as fast as a phone call while providing a written record of your communication.

A growing number of members of Congress have e-mail. E-mail is not considered as important as letters, faxes, or phone calls, however. If you use e-mail, be sure to include your postal mailing address so it is clear that you reside in your member's district and to enable the office to send you a mailed response.

The best way to e-mail your congressional representatives is to go to their Web site and follow the instructions for contacting them by e-mail. You must be a constituent to use this method.

Resource Organizations

The following organizations provide a wealth of information on young people and the issues facing them. By doing a search on the Internet using the organization's exact name, you can access its Web site, which will provide you with current contact information.

- ***Advocates for Youth.*** This organization provides information on peer education, youth development, and youth-adult partnerships. It also provides excellent resources for actively involving young people in their own learning.
- ***At the Table.*** An online clearinghouse featuring a wealth of information about effectively involving youth in decision making.
- ***Catholic Relief Services (CRS).*** An organization of the United States Conference of Catholic Bishops (USCCB), CRS provides information and resources on justice and advocacy issues internationally.
- ***Catholic Campaign for Human Development (CCHD).*** An organization of the USCCB, CCHD provides information and resources on justice and advocacy issues in the United States.
- ***Children's Defense Fund.*** Provides resources on issues affecting young people and an annual report on "The State of America's Children."
- ***CYD Journal: Community Youth Development.*** Dedicated to voicing progressive, humane, and caring approaches to harnessing the power of youth to affect community development. Similarly, encourages communities to embrace their role in the development for youth.
- ***National 4-H Council.*** 4-H is known for its lengthy history of fostering youth-adult partnerships in a variety of different projects.
- ***National Federation for Catholic Youth Ministry (NFCYM).*** As the national network for diocesan offices of youth ministry and collaborating organizations, NFCYM provides information on youth issues and resources for the development of youth ministry.

- ***National Study on Youth and Religion.*** Provides the most complete analysis of the religious practices and beliefs of American teenagers and information on issues affecting young people.
- ***Search Institute.*** Known for promoting forty developmental assets necessary for healthy adolescent development, the Search Institute conducts research and creates resources, including several resources on youth-adult partnerships, youth development, and mentoring.
- ***SoundOut.*** A national, nonprofit education program that works with elementary, middle, and high school students, teachers, and administrators to promote student voices in schools.
- ***UNICEF: The United Nations Children's Fund.*** UNICEF works for children's rights—their survival, development, and protection—through education, advocacy and fund-raising, guided by the "Convention on the Rights of the Child." They have an excellent youth-voices Web page that captures youth issues worldwide.
- ***Youth Activism Project.*** This national nonprofit is a clearinghouse that provides help and information to parents, mentors, teachers, principals, policy makers, and other adult allies who want to collaborate with youth to achieve positive community change. The organization provides a listing of more than one hundred national organizations, divided by topic areas that can assist in advocacy efforts.
- ***Youth Leadership Institute.*** An organization that provides information for training youth leaders, adult allies, and the systems that support them.

Acknowledgments

The scriptural quotations contained herein are from the New Revised Standard Version of the Bible, Catholic Edition. Copyright © 1993 and 1989 by the Division of Christian Education of the National Council of the Churches of Christ in the United States of America. All rights reserved.

The three goals on page 11 and the excerpts on pages 12, 21, and 73–74 are from *Renewing the Vision: A Framework for Catholic Youth Ministry*, by the United States Catholic Conference (USCC) (Washington, DC: USCC, 1997), pages 9, 11, 15, 27, 27–28, 27, and 27, respectively. Copyright © 1997 by the USCC, Inc.

The seven principles of Catholic social teaching on pages 19–20 are from *Sharing Catholic Social Teaching: Challenges and Directions, Reflections of the U.S. Catholic Bishops*, by the United States Conference of Catholic Bishops (USCCB) (Washington, DC: USCCB, 1999), pages 4–6. Copyright © 1999 by the USCCB. All rights reserved.

The material in the bullet list on pages 30–31 is from "Youth Involvement in Prevention Programming," found on the Advocates for Youth Web site, *www.advocatesforyouth.org*, accessed August 15, 2006.

The three styles on pages 33–34 and resource 2–A are adapted from "The Spectrum of Attitudes: Building a Theory of Youth Development," by Bill Lofquist, in *New Designs for Youth Development*, 5(3), 3–6, Fall 1989. Used with permission.

The youth ladder of participation information on pages 35–39 is from *Innocenti Essays*, number 4, *Children's Participation from Tokenism to Citizenship*, by Roger A. Hart (Florence, Italy: UNICEF Innocenti: Research Centre, 1992), page 8. Copyright © 1992 by UNICEF International Child Development Centre. Used with permission.

The inventory material on resource 2–A is adapted from *Making It Work: A Guide to Successful Youth-Adult Partnerships*, produced through a joint partnership of the Texas Network of Youth Services and the Prevention and Early Intervention/Community Youth Development Division of the Texas Department of Protective and Regulatory Services, pages 17–18, and found at *www.tnoys.org/TNOYSServices/PromptingYouthDev/Youth%20Adult%20Partnership%20Guide.pdf*, accessed January 18, 2007. Copyright © 2002. Used with permission

The material on resource 2–B is adapted from the paper "Adults as Allies," by Barry Checkoway (Dearborn, MI: School of Social Work, University of Michigan, 2004).

To view copyright terms and conditions for Internet materials cited here, log on to the home pages for the referenced Web sites.

During this book's preparation, all citations, facts, figures, names, addresses, telephone numbers, Internet URLs, and other pieces of information cited within were verified for accuracy. The authors and Saint Mary's Press staff have made every attempt to reference current and valid sources, but we cannot guarantee the content of any source, and we are not responsible for any changes that may have occurred since our verification. If you find an error in, or have a question or concern about, any of the information or sources listed within, please contact Saint Mary's Press.

"*Be a Champion of Youth: Standing With, By, and For Young People* is a must for anyone working with young people! It is an easy read that helps to sift through the many ways of ministering through advocacy. Getting young people involved in advocacy is made more accessible through the plain language and real-world examples used in this book. Worksheets and resources give youth workers practical tools to identify the need for advocacy and determine the best way to plan a successful campaign. Kudos to the McCartys for producing a valuable and much-needed resource!"

—Becki Kaman, coordinator of youth ministry
Saint Francis of Assisi, Fulton, MD

"Advocating with and for youth is an integral component of comprehensive youth ministry. Defining the term *advocacy* and acting on the concept is one of the greater challenges of working with young people. How do we integrate advocacy into ministry? What do we need to understand about structures and systems to empower teens to speak out? How do we focus our attentions on those issues that impact teens and communities?

"*Be a Champion of Youth: Standing With, By, and For Young People* defines advocacy in concrete terms. In addition, advocacy is examined in light of the Scriptures and Catholic Tradition. Instruments for assessing and evaluating mind-sets and efforts provide insights into current advocacy work. Inspiring examples of successful actions, ideas for helping youth find their own voices, a plan for building collaborative relationships with community organizations, and a vision for infusing advocacy into our parish and civic communities make this book a valuable resource for youth leaders, parish communities, and anyone who cares for and works with the young Church."

—Mary Kelly Mueller, coordinator of youth ministry
Good Shepherd Parish, Shawnee, KS